25/3/16

Rod,

Guaranteed no

Running contained.

Ian

You can never take what you love too seriously...

The Periodic Table Series

Periodically, we're all geeks about the things we love and the Periodic Table Series has been created to celebrate this universal fact.

Inspired by The Periodic Table of Chemical Elements*, our experts have applied scientific logic to an eclectic range of subjects that regularly baffle beginners and fire-up fans. The outcome of this experiment is the essential guide you hold in your hand.

Geeky? Absolutely.
Hugely satisfying? Categorically.

*The Periodic Table of Chemical Elements orders all the known matter that makes up our world, from hydrogen to helium, by chemical properties and behaviour to give scientists a handy overview of a rather complex subject.

For Helen and Spike

THE PERIODIC TABLE OF
HEAVY ROCK

IAN
GITTINS

EBURY
PRESS

10 9 8 7 6 5 4 3 2 1

Ebury Press, an imprint of Ebury Publishing,
20 Vauxhall Bridge Road,
London, SW1V 2SA

Ebury Press is part of the Penguin Random House
group of companies whose addresses can be found
at global.penguinrandomhouse.com

Penguin
Random House
UK

First published by Ebury Press in 2015

www.eburypublishing.co.uk

A CIP catalogue record for this book is available
from the British Library

ISBN: 978 1 785 03165 6

Printed and bound in China by Toppan Leefung

Penguin Random House is committed to a
sustainable future for our business, our readers
and our planet. This book is made from Forest
Stewardship Council® certified paper.

MIX
Paper from
responsible sources
FSC
www.fsc.org   FSC® C018179

Contents

The Periodic Table of
HEAVY ROCK

REACTIVE   TRANSITION   COMBUSTIBLE   ELEMENTAL   FERROUS

←

1 — **91** H — Hole

2 — **89** N — Nirvana
8 — **88** Ja — Jane's Addiction

3 — **95** Ff — Foo Fighters
9 — **92** Rg — Rage Against the Machine
23 — **69** Ch — Crazy Horse

4 — **91** Pj — Pearl Jam
10 — **98** Qs — Queens of the Stone Age
14 — **85** Fn — Faith No More
16 — **81** Bf — Black Flag
20 — **69** Mc — MC5
24 — **67** Bi — Big Brother & the Holding Company
28 — **69** Gf — Grand Funk Railroad
32 — **70** Bs — Black Sabbath
36 — **69** Lz — Led Zeppelin

5 — **90** Ai — Alice in Chains
11 — **88** P — Pixies
15 — **84** Rp — Red Hot Chili Peppers
17 — **83** M — Minor Threat
21 — **69** Sg — Stooges
25 — **71** Zt — ZZ Top
29 — **72** Bo — Blue Öyster Cult
33 — **67** Vf — Vanilla Fudge
37 — **65** Y — Yardbirds

6 — **88** So — Soundgarden
12 — **85** Dj — Dinosaur Jr.
18 — **88** Dz — Danzig
22 — **68** Bc — Blue Cheer
26 — **67** Ty — Ten Years After
30 — **69** Ab — Allman Brother Band
34 — **69** F — Free
38 — **68** Jb — Jeff Beck Group

7 — **91** Sp — Smashing Pumpkins
13 — **87** Mv — Melvins
19 — **82** Ba — Bad Brains
27 — **68** S — Steppenwolf
31 — **73** Ls — Lynyrd Skynyrd
35 — **68** Dp — Deep Purple
39 — **74** Bd — Bad Company

BASE METALS: ANCIENT

89 — **75** Dc — AC/DC
90 — **77** Mh — Motörhead
91 — **72** Sc — Scorpions
92 — **75** Ra — Rainbow
93 — **83** Di — Dio
94 — **78** Wh — Whitesnake
95 — **75** Tn — Ted Nugent

BASE METALS: MODERN

104 — **83** Me — Metallica
105 — **85** Mg — Megadeth
106 — **84** An — Anthrax
107 — **83** Sr — Slayer
108 — **87** Na — Napalm Death
109 — **90** Cc — Cannibal Corpse
110 — **94** Cf — Cradle of Filth

ELEMENT KEY
TOP LEFT: ELEMENT NUMBER
TOP RIGHT: YEAR OF FIRST RELEASE

								Bj 82/84 — Bon Jovi
			U 52/70 — UFO	**J** 58/75 — Journey	**Ae** 64/73 — Aerosmith	**Qu** 70/73 — Queen	**Gu** 76/87 — Guns N' Roses	**Mö** 83/81 — Mötley Crüe
			Ys 53/69 — Yes	**Fr** 59/77 — Foreigner	**K** 65/74 — Kiss	**Ny** 71/73 — New York Dolls	**Mm** 77/94 — Marilyn Manson	**R** 84/84 — Ratt
Jh 40/67 — Jimi Hendrix Experience	**W** 44/65 — Who	**Ru** 48/74 — Rush	**E** 54/70 — Emerson, Lake & Palmer	**Ro** 60/71 — REO Speedwagon	**Ac** 66/69 — Alice Cooper	**Ts** 72/82 — Twisted Sister	**Sx** 78/77 — Sex Pistols	**Pn** 85/86 — Poison
Rs 41/64 — Rolling Stones	**D** 45/66 — Doors	**Ib** 49/68 — Iron Butterfly	**G** 55/69 — Genesis	**Bt** 61/76 — Boston	**Db** 67/73 — David Bowie	**Sw** 73/71 — Sweet	**Dm** 79/77 — Damned	**Wp** 86/84 — W.A.S.P.
B 42/63 — Beatles	**Pf** 46/67 — Pink Floyd	**Gd** 50/67 — Grateful Dead	**Ta** 56/69 — Tangerine Dream	**Sy** 62/72 — Styx	**Mt** 68/69 — Mott the Hoople	**Sl** 74/69 — Slade	**Cu** 80/84 — Cult	**St** 87/84 — Spinal Tap
Cm 43/66 — Cream	**Ha** 47/70 — Hawkwind	**Vg** 51/69 — Van der Graaf Generator	**Kc** 57/69 — King Crimson	**A** 63/82 — Asia	**Ml** 69/77 — Meat Loaf	**Qa** 75/73 — Suzi Quatro	**Ds** 81/03 — Darkness	**Se** 88/09 — Steel Panther

Vh 96/78 — Van Halen	**Jp** 97/74 — Judas Priest	**Ir** 98/80 — Iron Maiden	**Dl** 99/80 — Def Leppard	**Sa** 100/79 — Saxon	**Ma** 101/82 — Manowar	**Gw** 102/88 — GWAR	**Av** 103/81 — Anvil
My 111/94 — Mayhem	**Rm** 112/95 — Rammstein	**Sk** 113/99 — Slipknot	**Pt** 114/83 — Pantera	**T** 115/93 — Tool	**Kn** 116/94 — Korn	**Lb** 117/97 — Limp Bizkit	**Td** 118/01 — Tenacious D

Introduction

Followers of that most determinedly self-aggrandising form of rock, heavy metal, are fond of defiantly proclaiming that 'metal never rusts'. For what it is worth, they are wrong. As any car owner knows, iron and its derivative compounds and alloys such as steel will rust in contact with oxygen and water. And every metal, save the most precious such as gold, eventually corrodes.

Still, no matter! Why should heavy rock fans, or musicians, be expected also to be scientifically well versed? When Neil Young wrote 'It's better to burn out than it is to rust', in 'My My, Hey Hey (Out Of The Blue)', it's unlikely his mind was on chemical decomposition formulae. When poor, doomed Kurt Cobain quoted the same song in his suicide note, his focus was figurative, not literal. Whatever Kurt was doing, he sure wasn't pondering chemical half-lives.

Metal is metal and science is science, and ne'er the twain shall meet – or shall they? Well, audacious undertaking as it may be, it makes a lot of sense to apply the structure and strictures of the Periodic Table to heavy rock. As every good high-school student knows, the table arranges each chemical element according to their properties and relationship to each other – dude, why should it not do the same for heavy rock?

Heavy rock is not just metal. Just as the Periodic Table racks up elements from the alkali metals on the left through to noble gases on the right, so heavy rock ranges from the first sixties psychedelic dreamers through ponderous progressive rock to modern bluesmen, pomp rockers, glam, punk, Goth, hardcore, hair metal and grunge rock. It's Hendrix *and* Hawkwind; Joplin *and* Judas Priest; MC5 *and* Meat Loaf. It's an extremely broad (if somewhat profane) church – and, as in chemistry, everything is interlinked.

Of course, unlike chemistry, heavy rock is not an exact science. This table is not definitive – it is a conversation-starter, a trigger for arguments. Some readers may well ask: where are the Animals, Creedence Clearwater Revival, the Clash, Opeth, Suicidal Tendencies or Sunn O)))? And what, exactly, they may continue, are the Beatles, David Bowie and guitar-free German electro pioneers Tangerine Dream doing in here?

They may be right – or they may not. Some artists dallied in heavy rock without devoting themselves to it. Others, such as Bowie, have exerted influence while only passing through. Heavy rock, its composition and its history are about more than riffs and volume, as this table reflects.

Did the Rolling Stones begat Aerosmith? How did the Pixies pave the way for Nirvana? Why are the Sex Pistols and the New York Dolls closely linked? Did Ozzy Osbourne and Black Sabbath accidentally invent death metal? And no matter how hard they try, are glam metal spoof act Steel Panther *really* as funny as Poison?

Questions, questions. This table may even have a few of the answers. So in the interests of chemical research, lets delve into rock's elemental matter. As Neil Young once also wrote, 'Keep on rocking in the free world!' But that was a crap song, with nothing to do with this book.

Reactive Metals

In the Periodic Table, reactive metals are the ones that respond the most intensely to the world around them. Some metals are impervious to chemical reactions; the reactive metals flame, corrode or transform when forced into contact with acids, water or oxidising agents.

When has heavy rock been so thin-skinned, so vulnerable to, and consumed by, the world around it? It is hard to see past the grunge rock scene that sprang up from America's north-west in the late 1980s and early 1990s. Volatile from the off, here was a music that appeared to be founded on chemical, and psychological, instability.

Throwing the urgency of punk and the sludgy grind of heavy metal into one plaid-shirted ball of disaffection, the Seattle bands rocked hard and heavy but their molecules were all awry. Like all reactive metals, they corroded and tarnished easily when removed from laboratory conditions.

The grunge movement's unwilling figurehead, Kurt Cobain, famously and tragically imploded and self-destructed under the pressure of fame, but he was not alone: his peers had far more than their fair share of their own chemical addictions, meltdowns and crises. There is only one major divergence: reactive metals have an extraordinary ability to absorb heat.

This bunch didn't.

Column 1

1 H 91 Hole	
2 N 89 Nirvana	**8 Ja 88** Jane's Addiction
3 Ff 95 Foo Fighters	**9 Rg 92** Rage Against the Machine
4 Pj 91 Pearl Jam	**10 Qs 98** Queens of the Stone Age
5 Ai 90 Alice in Chains	**11 P 88** Pixies
6 So 88 Soundgarden	**12 Dj 85** Dinosaur Jr.
7 Sp 91 Smashing Pumpkins	**13 Mv 87** Melvins

HOLE

The lightest element in the Periodic Table, hydrogen is also hugely combustible and flammable. It figures that H stands not just for hydrogen, but also for Hole. Fiercely incendiary, Courtney Love has rarely seen an argument that she doesn't want to jump into. Hole always sounded as if they were spoiling for a fight – and they had plenty to choose from.

Heavy rock has never been an equal opportunities employer: this Periodic Table is inevitably largely composed of hirsute geezers who know their way around a guitar amp. Love met with incalculable amounts of sexism and chauvinism. She was already a veteran of brief spells in Babes in Toyland and Faith No More when she founded Hole, and in 1991 they released their debut *Pretty On The Inside*, a raw howl of cathartic rage and frustration set to a rudimentary punk-metal thrash.

It was a cool enough of-its-time hard-rock record, yet Love was catapulted into the global spotlight over the tumultuous next couple of years as grunge exploded across the globe, she married Kurt Cobain, and the pair became parents and faced accusations of hard drug use before Cobain blew his head off with a shotgun on 5 April 1994.

Four days later came the release of Hole's second album, the appositely titled *Live Through This*. It was a sharp, tremendous album, with Love's righteous feminist rage and idiosyncratic mix of audacious entitlement and self-doubt battling each other across tracks such as 'Miss World' and the brilliant, lacerating 'Doll Parts'.

Inevitably, though, even as Love fought to cope with the devastating loss of her husband, press vultures circled claiming that she was an evil opportunist; a talent-free gold-digger; that Cobain must have written the album. The public vitriol aimed towards a grieving widow was shameful, and while Hole never again scaled the artistic or commercial heights of *Live Through This*, it's to Love's immense credit that she stuck around to try.

Hole deserve to be top of this Periodic Table not because of Courtney Love's infamy, or due to her legendary late husband, but because this great band rocked like bastards.

2	89
N	
Nirvana	

NIRVANA

Next to hydrogen in the Periodic Table lies lithium – used in the treatment of bipolar disorder, and consequently an element that Kurt Cobain knew well: he even wrote a song about it. It is also highly reactive – and has any rock band striven for such purity, burned so intensely, proven so fatally unstable and imploded as cataclysmically as did Nirvana? Theirs was a terrible and salutary tale, rendered all the heart-rending for playing out in the unblinking glare of celebrity and the global media.

There is little doubt that Kurt Cobain was happiest as a geeky Seattle rock fan, fixating on his favourite artists such as the Pixies, Neil Young and the Meat Puppets; playing in punk bands like Fecal Matter and the Stiff Woodies; roadie-ing for local sludge metallers the Melvins. When he formed Nirvana with bassist Krist Novoselic, they signed to Sub Pop and put out a decent-but-no-more 1989 debut album, *Bleach*.

So far, so unremarkable. After drummer Dave Grohl arrived, what Cobain never expected was for Nirvana's 1991 second album, *Nevermind*, to crash into the mainstream, wrestle Michael Jackson from atop the Billboard chart, go multi-platinum and become the voice of a generation (X, as it happened). It would have shaken the strongest individual and Cobain – troubled, contrary and punk-indie to his core, still covering Vaselines songs and producing Melvins albums – was not the strongest individual.

An attempt to retreat back to the indie margins by hiring Steve Albini to produce Nirvana's next album, *In Utero*, failed, and the rest is tragedy. Allergic to celebrity, recoiling from the demands and the banality of fame, Cobain sank into heroin abuse and manic depression before his inevitable suicide. His suicide note turned to Neil Young: 'It's better to burn out than to fade away.' Even in death, for Kurt Cobain, it was all about the music.

FOO FIGHTERS

When a chemical element loses an electron, it can change that element's properties entirely. When a rock band loses a member, the transformation is equally radical – especially if that member is the songwriter, front man and a global icon.

Dave Grohl freely confesses that he spent the year after Kurt Cobain's suicide doing nothing, unable even to look at a drum kit – and yet has bounced back to form one of the world's biggest heavy-rock groups, a stadium-filling draw across the globe. He has done so by reproducing yet also toning down the trademark Nirvana sound, and allying that band's frenetic punk-metal with pop hooks and melodies that float and sting.

Much as sodium lacks hydrogen's volatility, Foo Fighters lack Nirvana's desperate yearning and cathartic edge, but they are also far less likely to frighten radio programmers, and have consequently enjoyed success way beyond Cobain's reach or, indeed, desire. Their career to date is the obverse of Nirvana's: where Cobain's band burst into the stratosphere with precipitous haste, leaving their fragile front man unprepared and vulnerable, Foo Fighters have plugged away, a slow build, releasing an album pretty much every two years for two decades, finally having a US number 1 album with their seventh release, 2011's *Wasting Light*.

Nor have they done it by selling out their founding principles and embracing bland arena rock: beneath the occasional sugar-coated pop hits, Grohl's men still rock hard and as venomously: hence his part-time gigs in Queens of the Stone Age and blues-metal supergroup Them Crooked Vultures.

Ultimately, it's a difference not down to chemistry but to character. Foo Fighters have achieved world domination with a seemingly permanent smile plastered across their front man's face. Unlike Kurt Cobain, being a rock star does not kill Dave Grohl: it makes him stronger.

PEARL JAM

4   91
Pj
Pearl Jam

Grunge was eagerly painted as being all about the shock of the new, but there was plenty coming out of Seattle and its environs in the early 1990s that sounded both very familiar and highly enjoyable to hard rock and classic rock fans.

Pearl Jam are the classic example. Influenced not only by Led Zeppelin's heavyweight machinations but also the reedy drawl of Neil Young and the propulsion of the Who, the band that emerged from the ashes of Mother Love Bone after the OD of their singer Andrew Wood loomed on to the radar seemingly fully formed with their 1992 debut album, *Ten*.

Unlike Nirvana, Pearl Jam didn't represent an iconoclastic rejection of the crunching yet melodic arena rock of the 1970s: indeed, tracks like 'Jeremy' continued that venerable tradition. *Ten* outsold *Nevermind* and their follow-up, 1994's *Vs*, hit number 1 on the Billboard chart, causing the punkier, more entrenched grunge-rock fans to accuse Pearl Jam of careerism.

This was harsh: despite their stellar success, they retained the ideological purity of hardcore punks like Black Flag as a strong trace element in their chemical make-up. Singer Eddie Vedder frequently appears as uncomfortable with fame and celebrity as did Kurt Cobain, but where the Nirvana man self-destructed under the pressure, Vedder has taken a more proactive, socially engaged route, attempting to play small venues as well as stadiums and enormo-domes, accusing Ticketmaster in court of forcing up gig prices, and quietly giving hundreds of thousands of dollars to charities and liberal good causes.

Pearl Jam have now lumbered on for close on 25 years, veering between punk-metal and arty arena rock and selling 60 million albums along the way. Yet strip away this veneer and they remain at heart an idealistic, driven punk band.

ALICE IN CHAINS

Unlike chemistry, the world of heavy rock is prone to chance and feats of random happenstance. Alice in Chains would in all likelihood be lying happily in the base-metals subsection of this Periodic Table, had they not come from Seattle. Their debut album, 1990's *Facelift*, was a dour, grinding affair that owed as much to Black Sabbath or to Deep Purple as it did more leftfield, contemporary entities: they were a metal band through and through, as they proved by touring not just with Iggy Pop, but also Van Halen and even Poison.

Yet when Nirvana soared into the stratosphere with *Nevermind*, Alice in Chains were pulled in their wake, with their major record label keen to push them towards the hipper, more indie-inclined kids who couldn't get enough of all things Seattle. The strategy worked, but Alice in Chains had other things on their mind: founder and singer Layne Staley was sinking deep into heroin addiction.

This sorry situation appeared to be the sole subject matter of the band's second album, 1992's *Dirt*, as evidenced by its soul-baring song titles: 'Down In A Hole', 'Sickman', 'Junkhead', 'God Smack'. Likewise, musically the sludge metal of *Dirt* sounded weary, jaded, self-disgusted, but the Seattle frenzy lifted it into the Billboard top 10.

Its self-titled 1995 follow-up did even better, hitting number 1 despite exhibiting little musical or lyrical progression, but Staley's debilitating condition meant Alice in Chains were unable to tour, and they released no further material before his overdose death in 2002. They were to re-form in 2009 with a new singer, William DuVall, and no notable alteration in their sound: as ever, they sound like doom metallers who gatecrashed a party they never quite fitted in at.

6	88
So	
Soundgarden	

SOUNDGARDEN

Grunge rock's detractors liked to claim that it was basically hoary old heavy metal dressed in a plaid shirt, and while this accusation was a gross over-simplification, it rang true with Alice in Chains... and with Soundgarden.

Unlike Nirvana, with their love for the Sex Pistols and the Pixies, Soundgarden were grounded firmly in the epic blues of Led Zeppelin and the morose grind of Black Sabbath. They were certainly part of the early, fast-evolving Seattle story: they released their first EP on the fledgling Sub Pop before shifting to Black Flag's SST label for their 1988 debut album, *Ultramega OK*.

Yet unlike Nirvana, with their self-doubt and precocious musical nuances, Soundgarden always sounded as if they were trying to hold themselves back from covering 'Stairway To Heaven', an impression confirmed by 1991's *Badmotorfinger* album, despite its sporadic art-rock twists and uneven time signatures. They fully crossed the Rubicon on 1994's *Superunknown*, a colossal, crashing riff frenzy from which all traces of punk insurrection had been eschewed in favour of Zeppelin-style portentousness, as exemplified by their best-known track, 'Black Hole Sun'. It was a long way from Sub Pop, but the US public loved the band's heavier, meatier incarnation and sent *Superunknown* straight to number 1.

Yet when you get to the top the only way is down, and the 1996 follow-up *Down On The Upside* was an example of diminishing returns, again majoring on their characteristic gnarly metal riffs and brooding, non-specific angst but with far less originality or inspiration. It went platinum but sold less than a fifth of what its predecessor had and Soundgarden duly split, not to reunite for 14 years.

Soundgarden were heavy, sure: they were also very lucky to be in the right place at the right time.

SMASHING PUMPKINS

Although the Smashing Pumpkins are regarded as staples of the early 1990s US alternative-rock explosion, it is arguable that the only quality they shared with the Seattle grunge bands was Billy Corgan's solipsism.

Where Nirvana were guided by hardcore punk's idealism and DIY ethos, and Soundgarden and Alice in Chains were basically metal bands hitching a ride, the Smashing Pumpkins were expansive, far nearer in spirit to progressive rockers like Pink Floyd than they were to Pearl Jam. The Pumpkins started off paying at least lip service to the notion of being a punk-influenced band by signing to Sub Pop, but quickly moved on and by 1993's *Siamese Dream* were being truer to their instincts and crafting full on angst-ridden, episodic pop-metal symphonies.

Even this was a mere *amuse-bouche* next to 1995's *Mellon Collie And The Infinite Sadness*, a wildly pretentious two-disc, two-hour prog-rock sprawl that, for all its sporadic guttural grunge guitars, belonged on a 1975 edition of *The Old Grey Whistle Test* bookended by Emerson, Lake & Palmer and Queen. Yet its killer singles, including 'Bullet With Butterfly Wings' and 'Tonight, Tonight', fired it to number 1 in the US.

From then on, the Smashing Pumpkins became largely a vehicle for Corgan's soaring ego, turning in hard-rock workouts and concept pieces as he saw fit. In 2008, as the sole remaining original member of the band, he decided to record a 44-track concept album, *Teargarden By Kaleidyscope*, inspired by Tarot cards, releasing each track as a free download as he finished it – a project that Spinal Tap might have baulked at. The Smashing Pumpkins may be weighty but they're also, now and then, highly ridiculous.

Transition Metals

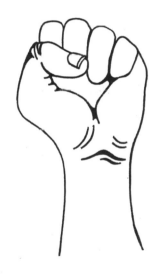

The early 1990s grunge bands shared many metaphysical qualities – attitude, politics, self-sufficiency – with the US hardcore bands of a decade earlier. They did not, however, sound a great deal like them: their antecedents' influence had been filtered through groups acting as transition metals.

Transition metals are ductile, malleable and conduct heat and electricity. Primarily, they bond with other elements as they alter their molecular structures. Put simply, the Stooges may never have begat Nirvana had they not passed through the Pixies.

These transition bands took the polemical politicking and guitar thrash of Black Flag and Minor Threat and rendered them accessible, theatrical, showbiz. Rage Against the Machine translated their anti-establishment agenda into slick slogans and buzzwords; the Red Hot Chili Peppers ripped off Bad Brains's choppy funk/reggae hardcore template wholesale.

Transition metals are shiny and gaudy, and Jane's Addiction and Faith No More certainly glistened under the hot stage lights. They are also the only elements that can produce a magnetic field, and from Anthony Kiedis to Perry Farrell to Zack de la Rocha, these phosphorescent groups manifest a classic, essential heavy-rock quality: magnetic front men.

Column 2

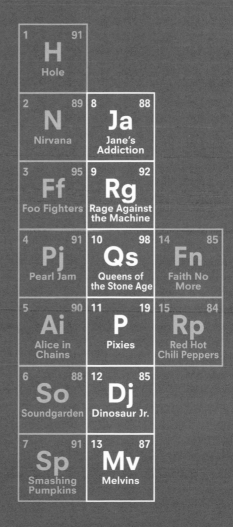

1 91 **H** Hole		
2 89 **N** Nirvana	**8** 88 **Ja** Jane's Addiction	
3 95 **Ff** Foo Fighters	**9** 92 **Rg** Rage Against the Machine	
4 91 **Pj** Pearl Jam	**10** 98 **Qs** Queens of the Stone Age	**14** 85 **Fn** Faith No More
5 90 **Ai** Alice in Chains	**11** 19 **P** Pixies	**15** 84 **Rp** Red Hot Chili Peppers
6 88 **So** Soundgarden	**12** 85 **Dj** Dinosaur Jr.	
7 91 **Sp** Smashing Pumpkins	**13** 87 **Mv** Melvins	

JANE'S ADDICTION

Jane's Addiction are one of the most inflammable, volatile elements in this table, and their exact place in the chemical spectrum is open to debate. Some observers would place them at the opposite end of the table, given that they were clearly partly shaped by the showy, anarchic theatrics of the likes of the Sex Pistols and the burlesque noir of Alice Cooper.

Nevertheless, Jane's Addiction belong down this more authenticity-hungry end of the table because of their vast influence on early 1990s US alternative rock (Tom Morello of Rage Against the Machine sees them as 'as important as Nirvana') and their founding of the Lollapalooza festival headlined by the likes of Pearl Jam, Soundgarden and Alice in Chains.

Front man Perry Farrell is a gadfly, a bohemian agent provocateur, a shock tactician never happier than when, for example, decreeing that Jane's Addiction's major-label debut album, 1988's *Nothing's Shocking*, should be housed in a sleeve depicting a sculpture of two naked women on fire that led to it being banned in some outlets.

The bacchanalian Jane's had no truck with the straight-edge puritanism of grunge's more fundamentalist operatives: they have always embraced funk, jazz and even folk tropes. Live, their arty, hard-hitting, testosterone-driven carnival evokes Red Hot Chili Peppers; it's no coincidence that members have ricocheted back and forth between the two bands.

Ultimately, Jane's Addiction are the rarest, most precious of chemical compounds: an art-rock band with the emphasis lying equally heavy on both syllables.

RAGE AGAINST THE MACHINE

Arriving as grunge neared its peak moment, the polemical rap-rock crossover troupe Rage Against the Machine drew heavily on the social activism and militancy of 1980s US hardcore punks such as Minor

Threat and the showmanship of Jane's Addiction and the Red Hot Chili Peppers.

Hip hop and funk can be deal-breakers for hidebound heavy-rock fans, yet Rage managed to infiltrate these elements into their wildly disaffected, obsessively establishment-baiting protest music. Guitarist Tom Morello machine-gunned out rancorous, gymnastic riffs with a serious grudge as vocalist Zack de la Rocha sang, rapped and itemised his limitless grievances against Western corporatism and the inequities of late-period capitalism.

What were Rage angry about? How long have you got? Their tumultuous self-named 1992 debut album fired impeccable leftist, pseudo-revolutionary broadsides on all fronts. A charged assault on societal ills, it spawned hits in the UK (but not the US) including signature tune 'Killing In The Name'. This hyperventilating, incandescent-with-ire denunciation of The System and The Man, with its bawled, stuttering chorus 'Fuck you, I won't do what you tell me!' was easily mocked as adolescent truculence (now-defunct weekly music paper *Melody Maker* memorably retitled it 'Fuck you, I won't tidy my bedroom!') but was undoubtedly thrilling.

Rage took four years to produce a follow-up album, the US number 1 *Evil Empire*, whose rap-metal fusion was equally vehement even if the politics of 'Bulls On Parade' and 'Vietnow' were a mix of cartoon over-simplification and bug-eyed conspiracy theory. Yet by now RATM weren't just heavy, they were huge, with their third album *The Battle Of Los Angeles* also topping the Billboard chart.

Doubtless fatigued by their 24/7 anger and earnestness, de la Rocha then quit, claiming that the band itself had become anti-democratic, but in a grunge-dominated era of rock solipsism, Rage Against the Machine's bracing activism was a welcome chemical antidote.

10	98

Qs

Queens of
the Stone Age

QUEENS OF THE STONE AGE

Vast acclaim has long been heaped on Queens of the Stone Age, who for much of the twenty-first century have been the metal band that it is okay for indie kids and hipsters to like.

This coruscating, cryptic band began life as Kyuss, a legendary Californian group who would drive out to the Mojave Desert, take acid and jam deep into the night. When this source material evolved into Queens of the Stone Age, their self-named 1998 debut album hinted at the brute force and ferocious intelligence that was to come.

Their 2000 album *Rated R* was a masterpiece of finger-shredding guitar riffs, labyrinthine Led Zeppelin-like rhythms and powerhouse percussion, yet leavened with irony and humour, not least in its lead-off track 'Feel Good Hit Of The Summer', in which founder and singer Josh Homme itemised his chemical consumption of that particular evening: 'Nicotine, Valium, Vicodin, marijuana, ecstasy and alcohol… c-c-c-c-c-cocaine!'

On the album and its follow-up, 2002's *Songs For The Deaf* featuring Dave Grohl on drums and Screaming Trees's Mark Lanegan on guest vocals and guitar, QOTSA's musicianship was ferocious and expansive, but never intimidating or exclusive: the knowing half-smile around Homme's lips pulled you in to share their sardonic in-joke.

The mainstream caught on, with 2005's *Lullabies To Paralyze* album going top 5 in the US before Homme took time out to form the Them Crooked Vultures supergroup with Grohl and former Led Zeppelin bassist John Paul Jones: when he returned to QOTSA, 2013's *…Like Clockwork*, their first album in seven years, topped the Billboard chart.

What a journey. Harmonising with the album's special guest Elton John in the studio, the unflappable Homme must have felt as if he were still stoned in the Mojave.

11   88

P

Pixies

PIXIES

When the leader of the most significant heavy-rock band of the 1990s, Kurt Cobain, was asked to describe the musical roots of Nirvana, he answered: 'I was just trying to rip off the Pixies.' Dave Grohl has gone further, pinning them as being responsible for the 'quiet/ loud dynamic' that dominated US alternative music throughout the decade.

The Pixies were massively influential on the US hard-rock landscape – and yet somehow also oddly detached from it. For all of the ferocious noise the Boston foursome unleashed via jagged squalls of guitar, cataclysmic drums and the banshee howl of singer Black Francis, there was something nerdy about these ex-college kids' preoccupations with space aliens, sex and gratuitous, stylised violence. You could imagine them being into, like, Periodic Tables.

The Pixies borrowed from the sheer guitar rush of Hüsker Dü and Sonic Youth and the fantastical imagination of David Bowie but the resulting sonic carnage was very much their own. Despite the praise lauded on their twitchy 1988 debut album *Surfer Rosa*, produced in three weeks by hardcore noise aficionado Steve Albini, their highwater mark was the next year's follow-up, *Doolittle*.

Around guitars that crunched and rampaged enough for the most abandoned of heavy rockers, the Pixies stuttered out tales of gouging out eyeballs, driving cars into the ocean and of apocalyptic environmental woes in songs that ranted, raved and spoke in tongues – and in Spanish. It was a surrealist, sophisticated art-rock masterpiece that even charted top 10 in the UK.

It wasn't just Cobain and Grohl who were listening open-mouthed; outside of heavy rock, Radiohead were to confess that in their early years, the Pixies were the main, if not only, musical touchstone. Later years saw the Pixies head towards more conventional rock terrain before tensions between Francis and bassist Kim Deal led them to split, a fault line that was to resurface when they re-formed post-millennium. Yet they remain a vast shaping influence on this end of the Periodic Table: they were a brilliant, brilliant band.

DINOSAUR JR.

Despite being fronted by a man so laconic and diffident that he at times actually appeared to be amoebic, Dinosaur Jr. exerted a huge influence over US alternative and heavy rock in the late 1980s.

Formed in 1983 by singer and guitarist J. Mascis and originally called Dinosaur, after a patchy debut album they lengthened their name and upped their game in 1987 when they signed to Black Flag founder Greg Ginn's SST label and released *You're Living All Over Me*. It was a ground-breaking record, with its ragged, ramshackle yet oddly sturdy punk-pop anthems staggering beneath the weight of chiming guitar solos, 45-degree turns into white noise and freeform jams, and the reedy peal of Mascis's hesitant, defeated vocal.

There were traces of progressive rock, of grinding metal, even of faux-jazzy chord shifts, and it was a remarkably spirited performance by a man who, in person and interview, appeared so seized by torpor and apathy that it seemed he found it a chore to breathe in and out. The following year's *Bug* gave alt-rock its 1988 national anthem in 'Freak Scene', a blast of ragged white noise with killer hooks and chorus, and even earned Dinosaur Jr. a major deal.

Having taken Nirvana on tour as their support act in 1991, Mascis's band looked perfectly placed to benefit as the heavy-rock and indie worlds alike went Seattle-crazy, but as ever they stuck resolutely to their low-key guns, unwilling to write 'Smells Like Teen Spirit'-style crowd-pleasing anthems and preferring to hone their Neil Young-meets-noise-rock shtick.

By now Dinosaur Jr. were purely a vehicle for Mascis: when he split the band in 1998 to record under his own name, you could not see the join. He has ambled on ever since, a rogue chemical element who triggered a seismic rock reaction.

MELVINS

Heavyweight both in musical density and reputation, it is nevertheless impossible to view the Melvins as anything other than leaden and lumpen. While their commercial success was negligible, the Seattle band have attained legendary status in grunge rock lore for their large influence on a wide-eyed, teenage Kurt Cobain, who roadied for them pre-Nirvana.

Formed in 1985 in Cobain's hometown of Aberdeen, the Melvins have ever since majored in glacially paced, monolithic sludge metal, heavily borrowing from the first swamp-like stirrings of Black Sabbath. Yet they left their grimy mark on grunge, being a major shaping factor on the subterranean guitar grind of Nirvana, Soundgarden and Mudhoney (who included an ex-Melvins bassist, Matt Lukin). However, their own dreary, club-footed rock utterly lacked the yearning, wit and dark poetry that Nirvana brought to their angst-ridden art.

The Melvins were briefly on a major label in the wake of their noted protégé's precipitous rise to fame, and Cobain co-produced their 1993 album, *Houdini*, but when even this global icon youth could not provide a fillip-by-association to their sales, the Melvins fell back to their indie comfort zone. They are not pretty but they are prolific, every year grinding out an album (or two) that is essentially interchangeable with every other.

Cobain loved their integrity, independence and utter disinterest in compromising with the mainstream, and certainly the Melvins have never sold out. However, there is generally a reason why things don't sell out: nobody wants to buy them.

Column 3

8 Ja **88** Jane's Addiction	
9 Rg **92** Rage Against the Machine	
10 Qs **98** Queens of the Stone Age	**14** Fn **85** Faith No More	**16** Bf **81** Black Flag
11 P **88** Pixies	**15** Rp **84** Red Hot Chili Peppers	**17** M **83** Minor Threat
12 Dj **85** Dinosaur Jr.		**18** Dz **88** Danzig
13 Mv **87** Melvins		**19** Ba **82** Bad Brains

14   85
Fn
Faith No
More

FAITH NO MORE

Art rock with a bad attitude is a reliably winning formula
and Faith No More were artier and sneerier than most.
From the off, their chemical bag was a potent mix of
metal, hard rock, funk and even hip hop as they worked
their way through an array of hopeful lead singers,
including a teenage Courtney Love.

For their first two albums of convulsive prog-metal
Chuck Mosley was on vocals, but Faith No More found
their arch, sardonic voice when Mike Patton replaced him
after a band coup. FNM had all the standard hard-rock
assault weapons of seizure-like rhythms, chugging guitar
detonations and seismic drumming in their arsenal, but
accessorised them with wildly eclectic influences from
hip hop to synth pop and a brutally sarcastic sense of
black humour.

Their first post-Mosley album, 1989's *The Real Thing*,
almost went top 10 in the US, as did its follow-up, 1992's
Angel Dust, where Patton's artier, more outré leanings
found expression via skew-whiff vocal stylings, distorted
samples and a foreboding, ominous cover of John Barry's
'Midnight Cowboy', of all things.

This was ironic yet heavyweight 1990s progressive
rock, yet Faith No More were as riven by tensions and
subtextual struggles as was their music, defenestrating
founding guitarist Jim Martin in the middle of the decade.
Martin's misanthropic presence was key to the group's
sound and character and their final two albums pared
back the arty weirdness and experimentation and upped
the melodicism.

Yet even melodic and restrained Faith No More
albums were more fucked up than 99 per cent of bands,
and it was a loss when they split in 1998. Inevitably, they
re-formed ten years on to tour the world's festivals and
even chanced a new album, *Sol Invictus*, in 2015, but the
world just wasn't as interested as it used to be.

15	84
Rp	
Red Hot Chili Peppers	

RED HOT CHILI PEPPERS

In rock, as in colonialism, the pioneers take the arrows and the settlers take the land. Bad Brains may have been the first US hardcore punks to leaven the genre's linear thrash with funk and reggae tropes, but it was the Red Hot Chili Peppers who honed this formula and rocketed to global arena-filling success.

This is not to imply they were mere opportunists: singer Anthony Kiedis, guitarist Hillel Slovak, bassist Flea and drummer Jack Irons had been infiltrating Parliament-style funk into Black Flag-like punk-metal ever since their grandly named teenage band, Tony Flow & the Miraculously Majestic Masters of Mayhem. Renamed as RHCP and signed to a major, George Clinton himself even produced their 1985 album *Freaky Styley*, but after Slovak's death from a heroin OD, it was 1989's *Mother's Milk* that saw them maximise the impact of their fibrillating funk and provocative hard rock.

By now, Red Hot Chili Peppers were as testosterone-driven and macho as the most hirsute metallers yet also possessed of a febrile funkiness and an odd vulnerability captured in the surprisingly poetic lyrics of the unexpectedly sensitive Kiedis. This unusual alchemy bewitched hard-rock fans and MTV-gawking pop kids alike, and world domination arrived via 1991's *Blood Sugar Sex Magik*, where their once ungainly funk-metal sounded sinewy, guttural and colossal.

Yet the Chili Peppers lost their mojo in the 1990s as guitarist John Frusciante, who had replaced Slovak, quit to fight his drug habit: when he returned to the band in 1999, their lush and panoramic *Californication* album cemented their position at the very apex of the heavy-rock world.

In the twenty-first century the Red Hot Chili Peppers appear to have fallen victim to hubris and bombast and to be about little more than size, as was exemplified by their sprawling, flatulent 2006 double album *Stadium Arcadium*. Yet their career remains a fine example of the dictum that the best heavy rockers always do more than *just* rock.

Combustible Metals

Many chemical elements are prone to combustion and explosion. In heavy rock, there are a handful of incandescent bands whose volatility appears to be their entire *raison d'être*.

The original human firework, Iggy Pop, was the first sinewy, evangelical Messiah of onstage spontaneous combustion, but he was not alone. His band the Stooges often shared a Detroit bill with their late 1960s rivals MC5, preaching their gospel of insurrection and revolution while striving to burst out of their skins.

That pair's agitation was to be a major musical influence on the American hardcore bands of the early 1980s, whose sonic excess and militant politicking amounted to a full-on assault on the senses: Minor Threat espoused a no-drink, no-drugs 'straight-edge' policy to maximise their powerhouse rush; Black Flag's Henry Rollins became a testosterone-fuelled, pumped-up attack weapon.

The animal ire and savage bile of these bands were to be a major influence on the likes of Red Hot Chili Peppers, Jane's Addiction, Faith No More and Rage Against the Machine. But these guys were the originals.

Column 4

14 **85** **Fn** Faith No More	**16** **81** **Bf** Black Flag	**20** **69** **Mc** MCs
15 **84** **Rp** Red Hot Chili Peppers	**17** **83** **M** Minor Threat	**21** **69** **Sg** Stooges
	18 **88** **Dz** Danzig	**22** **68** **Bc** Blue Cheer
	19 **82** **Ba** Bad Brains	

16	81
Bf	
Black Flag	

BLACK FLAG

The US hardcore punks of the 1980s took the orgiastic noise of MC5 and the Stooges and replaced the hedonism and self-destruction with self-control and societal awareness. Foremost among their number were Black Flag.

Formed in California in 1977 by guitarist Greg Ginn, they underwent numerous line-up changes before finding their definitive form when a bug-eyed fan, Henry Rollins, jumped on stage to sing with them at a New York gig. They promptly hired him.

When their major label rejected their debut album, 1981's *Damaged*, on grounds of bad taste and profanity, Ginn simply formed his own record label, SST, and released it himself. Tedious legal action inevitably followed.

When that had played itself out, Black Flag went into turbo-charged mode, putting out three albums in 1984 alone. Their music varied wildly, from demented garage rock with some serious bottom end, to jazzy experimental pieces, to frantic spoken-word political and personal rants and diatribes from Rollins.

This intensive eclecticism combined with their habit of living on the road, and apparently playing every single punk club and dive bar from California to Carolina, quickly gained Black Flag a fanatical cult following, a few of whom saw their gigs as a chance to take a swing at the belligerent and confrontational Rollins.

Black Flag chucked out two more albums in 1985 then split up the following year, worn out by their hyperactive schedule. The lifespan may have been brief but their legacy on what came next for US hard rock was huge, not least as Ginn's SST label was to nurture A-list alt-rockers such as Hüsker Dü, the Meat Puppets, Sonic Youth, Dinosaur Jr., Screaming Trees and Soundgarden.

For his part, Henry Rollins went on to become the most muscle-bound man in rock.

MINOR THREAT

These Washington, DC radical punks emerged close on five years after UK counterparts the Clash and the Sex Pistols, but they were purer in intent, integrity and lifestyle than their British precursors. Formed by vocalist Ian MacKaye in 1980 from the remains of school band the Teen Idles, Minor Threat strove for ideological perfection, eschewing alcohol and drugs and calling on their fans for constant mindfulness and self-improvement. They called it 'straight edge'.

MacKaye was the ultimate in the punk DIY ethos, having no truck with major labels and instead founding Dischord Records straight out of school to put out his music. In truth, there was not a lot to put out: after a flurry of early singles and EPs, Minor Threat released only one album, 1983's *Out Of Step*.

A bracing listen, it was characteristically short, sharp and shocking: the buzzsaw guitars and pummelling drums would grace any metal album, but were employed perfunctorily and judiciously on a mere eight tracks that seemed to be over before they had begun.

MacKaye's distaste for anything extraneous to his band's puritanical thrash extended to celebrity: when Minor Threat's constant touring and the good reception awarded to *Out Of Step* made him a noted figure on the alt-rock scene, he promptly broke up the band to focus on running his label. He was to return four years later with Fugazi, the band that took Minor Threat's ideals and wrote them large.

DANZIG

The singular Glenn Danzig is not so much an element in this Periodic Table as a one-man alloy of bizarre, seemingly contradictory elements, being equally beholden to the sharp, brittle hardcore punk of Black Flag and Minor Threat and the rocky-horror theatrics of Alice Cooper.

Danzig emerged in the late 1970s in the Misfits, basically a thrash-metal take on the Cramps's B-movie rock, passing through the relatively conventional metal band Samhain before striking out under his own name in 1987.

Throughout these manifestations, but particularly in his self-named band, he has veered between bluesy heavy metal with gothic styling, to apparent full-on attempts to summon the dark side via pulsing, atmospheric hard rock and lyrics that defy the sentient listener to keep a straight face.

This was certainly true on Danzig's self-named 1987 debut album with its potboiler tracks called things like 'Am I Demon', 'Possession' and 'Evil Thing' and even more so on 1990's *Lucifuge* with its chucklesome 'Snakes Of Christ' and 'Devil's Plaything'.

To their credit, the band spent their career trying to deepen and diversify their sound, moving away from common-or-garden metal towards romantic, melodramatic rock operas. Danzig even drew on quasi-classical music on *Black Aria*, a concept piece that attempted to tell the tale of Lucifer being banished from heaven via tracks like 'Retreat And Descent' and 'And The Angels Weep'.

It has never been clear how much Danzig, a man originally steeped in hardcore punk and whose band has included ex-members of Black Flag and Prong, actually believes all of this black-magic guff, especially in the later years when he took to naming albums *Blackacidevil* and *6:66 Satan's Child*. He clearly figured that even the thinking alt-rock demographic needed a daft Goth band – and he has filled that particular vacancy very adroitly.

BAD BRAINS

Reggae makes few incursions into the world of heavy rock, and thus into this table, but Bad Brains are the exception.

The Washington band were formed by jazz-fusion guitarist Gary Miller, aka Dr Know, as a deliberate attempt to meld the worlds of hardcore punk and reggae. It sounds the most toe-curlingly earnest and clunky genesis for a group but remarkably it worked, and their merger of ferocious Black Flag-like guitar exorcisms, fervid funk and righteous dub reggae earned them cult status on the US hardcore scene.

Their eponymous 1982 cassette-only debut album arguably represented the apotheosis of their audacious fusion, with its pulverising yet perfectly formed outbursts of ire such as 'Banned In DC' and 'Pay To Cum'. It's probable that some more hidebound hard-rock fans did a cartoon double take at black Rasta men playing adrenalin-fuelled aggravated punk rock, but Bad Brains were never a novelty act, and achieved the critical and near-impossible task of capturing the best of both of their music genres rather than merely diluting them.

Yet this balancing act was precarious, and after they signed to Greg Ginn's SST label, their prophetically titled 1986 third album *I Against I* found the band members pulling in different directions and rock elements swamping the reggae ones. Inevitably, the band's more hardline Rasta members, singer H.R. and drummer Earl Hudson, quit to revert to playing pure reggae. Dr Know recruited replacements, but after Bad Brains quit SST for a major label, their 1993 album *Rise* sounded like bog-standard thrash metal with token reggae rhythms phoned in.

Even when the original members reunited to sign to Madonna's Maverick label, the thrill had clearly gone – yet Bad Brains must have given a wry smile when they saw Red Hot Chili Peppers take their ahead-of-its-time musical formula and run with it all the way to the world's stadia, and banks.

Column 5

			23 69 **Ch** Crazy Horse
16 81 **Bf** Black Flag	20 69 **Mc** MCs	24 67 **Bi** Big Brother & the Holding Company	
17 83 **M** Minor Threat	21 69 **Sg** Stooges	25 71 **Zt** ZZ Top	
18 88 **Dz** Danzig	22 68 **Bc** Blue Cheer	26 67 **Ty** Ten Years After	
19 82 **Ba** Bad Brains		27 68 **S** Steppenwolf	

MC5

Like Jane's Addiction, MC5 could easily nestle at either end of this Periodic Table. Their incendiary, insurrectionary fervour and showmanship were clearly an influence on punks from the New York Dolls to the Sex Pistols, yet ultimately they belong at the weightier end of this spectrum for the sheer weightiness of their sonic terrorism.

For MC5, as with Blue Cheer and the Stooges, the noise came first. They were revolutionary in every way: just as their songs and stage rhetoric evangelistically called for rebellion and anarchy, so their music – rocket-fuelled, laden with feedback and reverb and both sleek and cranium-crushingly heavy – fought to burst free of all physical and spiritual constraints.

Guided by their counter-culture guru manager John Sinclair, who advocated societal overthrow via rock and roll, drugs and 'fucking in the streets', MC5 channelled their adolescent, inchoate rage into their brutish noise, wisely opting to make their 1969 debut album *Kick Out The Jams* a recording of a gig at the local Grande Ballroom in Detroit to attempt to capture the fire-and-brimstone magnificence of their live shows. It worked, thrillingly, with the adrenalin and amphetamine buzz of their onstage catharsis emphasising the ferocity and purity of their lyrical manifesto.

You can't keep that kind of intensity up for long and maybe MC5 were always going to be a brutishly brilliant flash in the pan: after Sinclair was jailed for drug possession they lost their way badly, recording an apolitical and sinewy yet rather aimless second album, *Back In The USA*, then sinking into a welter of drug addictions and bankruptcy and splitting in 1972. Yet from the ideological purity of Nirvana at one extreme of this table to the attitudinal showiness of Mötley Crüe at the other, a lot of bands owed a fuck of a lot to MC5.

21		69
	Sg	
	Stooges	

STOOGES

The Stooges got signed to their major record deal after being spotted supporting fellow Detroit rock-and-roll missionaries MC5 and they shared many features with these local kindred spirits. Yet where MC5's righteous rage was largely political, the Stooges' raw primitivism and boundary pushing was all about hedonism, narcotic adventuring and self-expression.

From the outset their music was a jarring, jagged marriage of truculent garage rock and mutated blues, while singer Iggy Pop took Jim Morrison's wild man posing to the nth degree of excess and absurdity live, slashing his torso with broken glass, debuting stage diving and putting himself in serious danger by challenging audiences of pissed bikers to a fight.

It was heavy in every way, yet it could have been a mere circus of the grotesque and a pointless art pantomime were it not backed up by the Stooges' powerhouse, potent rock songs. The classic self-named 1969 debut album yielded '1969', 'I Wanna Be Your Dog' and 'No Fun', three pulsating expressions of the adolescent nihilism that was always their motor and motivation.

Inevitably, Iggy's antics earned their live show a freak-show reputation, but they were undercut by a profound ache and existential aspiration/desperation that made the Stooges way more than hollow narcissists. Like MC5 and Blue Cheer, they were destined not to stick around: the noise freak-out of second album *Fun House* was a commercial disaster and Pop sank into heroin addiction.

Even an intervention by David Bowie, who produced the Stooges' third album, *Raw Power*, failed to stem the decline, despite it boasting feral assaults like 'Search And Destroy' and 'Gimme Danger'. Bowie was to take Iggy to Berlin and help him launch his (slightly) more measured solo career, yet the Stooges legacy on hard rock remains a blood-red, blistering scorch mark.

22   68
Bc
Blue Cheer

BLUE CHEER

A rogue particle in the chemical atmosphere, Blue Cheer existed for only five years but exerted an influence way greater than that measly duration might suggest.

Born in San Francisco in 1967, audibly in thrall to Jimi Hendrix and Cream, this power trio made such an almighty racket it seemed hardly credible that it could be generated by three mere mortals. Their secret was brilliantly simple: they were utterly reductive, paring the blues down to the most basic, dumbass riffs and rhythms imaginable, then blasting out this swampy mess draped in distortion and at ear-shattering volume.

Their formula was not unlike the one that Black Sabbath was to adopt a few thousand miles away, but unlike Sabbath, Blue Cheer's primal din was still clearly rooted in the Delta. Vocalist and bassist Dickie Peterson, guitarist Leigh Stephens and drummer Paul Whaley were far from accomplished players, but 1968 debut album *Vincebus Eruptum* compensated for any shortcomings in that area by the simple expedient of bludgeoning listeners into submission.

It was Hendrix minus the skyscraping imagination and versatility, MC5 without the amphetamine energy, or the Yardbirds with their R&B pulse in an ICU. Blue Cheer lacked most of the normal qualities manifested in heavy rock except for menace and malevolence, but their stagnant bitches' brew packed quite an aftertaste. Twenty years later, their malign influence was easily detectable in grunge pioneers such as the Melvins and Soundgarden.

With the exception of that debut album and a mangling of Eddie Cochran's 'Summertime Blues' that somehow went top 3 in the US, Blue Cheer had little chart success, and ground through numerous line-up changes before splitting in 1972. Yet they left their dark, gnarly legacy hanging over hard/progressive rock like a noxious, bizarrely compelling odour.

Elemental Metals

The phrase 'elemental metal' sounds distinctly oxymoronic. Yet where the uncultivated frenzy of MC5 or the Stooges, say, appeared to be random, savage acts willed into being by deviant creatures, elemental metal is more obviously a product of the soil. It is rooted, grounded, as if the music has sprung from the earth to be harvested by the artists.

The most common root of elemental metal is the blues. So many bands have built their musical edifice on that 12-bar Delta throb, ladling on power, volume and attitude to turn it into a rock detonation. Sometimes, as with Big Brother & the Holding Company, the defining USP is a human fireball.

ZZ Top filled the world's arenas playing amplified, homely old Texan bar blues. Boorish plodders Grand Funk Railroad and classic rock one-hit wonders Steppenwolf did similar. Deep South iconoclasts the Allman Brothers Band and Lynyrd Skynyrd factored in country music to satisfy their demographic of heavy-rock-loving good ol' boys.

Yet roots don't always imply restrictions: above and beyond this category floats the free spirit of Neil Young, surely the most questing, restless elemental metal of them all – and never more so than when aback Crazy Horse.

Column 6

	23 69 **Ch** Crazy Horse	
20 69 **Mc** MCs	**24 67** **Bi** Big Brother & the Holding Company	**28 69** **Gf** Grand Funk Railroad
21 69 **Sg** Stooges	**25 71** **Zt** ZZ Top	**29 72** **Bo** Blue Öyster Cult
22 68 **Bc** Blue Cheer	**26 67** **Ty** Ten Years After	**30 69** **Ab** Allman Brothers Band
	27 68 **S** Steppenwolf	**31 73** **Ls** Lynyrd Skynrd

NEIL YOUNG AND CRAZY HORSE

Famously, trying to pin down Neil Young is to try to corral water. The maverick Canadian has tried on virtually every musical genre extant for size during a uniquely idiosyncratic recording career fast nearing the half-century mark, but his most incandescent recordings are with Crazy Horse.

For years this raucous troupe seemed to serve as an escape route, a noisome comfort blanket for Young from the more mellow pleasures of Crosby, Stills, Nash and Young and his own acoustic-tinged country meanderings, but then the penny dropped: Crazy Horse was where he felt most at home and did his best work.

Over the decades, Young and his garage band have convened when the mood has taken him to make albums that have veered from dysfunctional folk-country to distorted, feedback-laden excursions into garage rock and white-noise existential laments.

At first meeting in 1969 they were rough and ready but fairly classicist. They branched out on later excursions such as 1975's intensive *Zuma*, 1978's ornery and abrasive *Rust Never Sleeps* and particularly the melodic yet menacing guitar maelstrom of *Ragged Glory* in 1989, a record that so rehabilitated Young's reputation that he went out on tour with New York art-rock hipsters Sonic Youth.

Yet Young and Crazy Horse's magnum opus came way later: a full 42 years after first picking up guitars together, they unloaded 2011's *Psychedelic Pill*, a 90-minute, nine-track double album whose sonic assaults and wanderings would have delighted fans of Hendrix, Zeppelin or any golden-age heavy-rock astral voyagers. A Dylan-like free spirit, Neil Young is one of those rare rockers who can fetch up in any box on this Periodic Table depending on his whim on the day.

BIG BROTHER & THE HOLDING COMPANY

24		67
	Bi	
Big Brother & the Holding Company		

There is no doubt about the primary element of Big Brother & the Holding Company's rock compound: they will forever be the band that gave the world the wracked, fervent, soul-baring howl of their force-of-nature singer Janis Joplin.

She actually, true to type, came late to the party: Big Brother were already established as a spirited if somewhat limited psychedelic-leaning bluesy Californian jam band when Joplin joined them in 1966, initially just as a co-lead singer. It did not take them long to realise that Joplin's heart-on sleeve, ferocious vocal performances could take them to another level entirely.

Joplin made their standard-issue bluesy, heavy-rock sound great, but in truth she could have made anything sound great: passionate, roaring as if possessed, frequently drunk and yet always miraculously tuneful, her live exorcisms made anybody who happened across her band comprehend they were In the presence of something very special indeed.

This was never truer than at 1967's Monterey Pop Festival, when her abandoned, impossibly soulful, gravel-throated testifying on 'Ball And Chain' utterly transfixed the afternoon crowd and enlightened thousands more to her extraordinary genius.

Tiresome record-label-contract shenanigans meant that Joplin and Big Brother only recorded one major-label album together, 1968's *Cheap Thrills*, but it was a belter, harnessing the band's valiant (but hardly virtuoso) progressive rock-blues workouts to Joplin's vivacious, yearning yowl. The record was to sell more than a million copies and hit number 1 in the US, as well as giving Joplin her first hit single in the fiery, insatiable 'Piece Of My Heart'.

No sooner had Joplin ascended to the stratosphere than she went solo, a decision that worked out neither for her nor for Big Brother: two years later she was dead from a heroin overdose and they had returned to obscurity.

25		71
	Zt	
	ZZ Top	

ZZ TOP

ZZ Top's heaviness has never been in question: nobody could doubt their devotion to hard-driving Texas barroom blues, not their proficiency in playing it. What is remarkable is how the Houston trio became not only popular but actual celebrities playing such rugged, unglamorous, non-poptastic music.

Their first two albums offered little evidence that they would break out of the Texas spit-and-sawdust boogie-blues circuit. However, 1973's *Tres Hombres* album climbed into the US top 10, and over the next decade ZZ Top became the biggest hard-rocking bar band in America.

Remarkably, they were to up the ante still further in 1983, as their *Eliminator* album spawned three global hit singles in 'Gimme All Your Lovin'', 'Sharp Dressed Man' and 'Legs': it was to sell more than 10 million albums in the US alone, earning an ultra-rare diamond sales classification.

Eliminator saw ZZ Top embrace synthesisers for the first time but not even the most hardline rock evangelist was yelling 'Judas!' at them: the spirit and the integrity of their music remained so palpably intact. The other reason for their unlikely success was that they turned themselves into a cartoon: despite their musical heaviness, they had never taken themselves terribly seriously, and their beards, Stetsons and knee-knocking 'dance' routines looked great on MTV.

They rode high into the 1990s, but familiarity eventually breeds contempt, and ZZ Top's fortunes declined until they were the latest veteran act to be rehabilitated by a Rick Rubin-produced comeback album, *La Futura*, in 2012. In truth, ZZ Top have never sounded like the future – strip away the production sheen of *La Futura* and it is not unlike their 42-year-old debut offering. Only the beards are greyer.

TEN YEARS AFTER

Rock and roll's chemistry lab can be a truly arbitrary place. Ten Years After might have been just another unremarkable British heavy-lifting barroom blues band if not for a career-making performance halfway down the bill at Woodstock festival.

Formed in Nottingham in 1967, their eponymous debut album was a bog-standard heavy-blues set, with the *de rigueur* mix of original material and Willie Dixon covers, enlivened only by the lightning riffs and virtuoso wizardry of lead singer and guitarist Alvin Lee. Their second album, the live set *Undead*, ended with a rollicking Lee-penned number called 'I'm Going Home', which was a minor US hit, leading to an invitation for them to appear at Woodstock.

When Ten Years After appeared at 8.15 on the Sunday evening (a full 12 hours before Jimi Hendrix's eventual headline set), Lee's blurred-finger guitar heroics on an extended jam of 'I'm Going Home' excited an ecstatic reaction and raised the profile of the previously scarcely known group sky high.

The band's next three albums consequently all reached the mid-to-lower reaches of the US top 20, although they were little more than efficient, speedy blues-metal sets weighed down by lyrics that veered from the lascivious to the ludicrous. It made it hard for them to cross over to anything other than the more reactionary wing of heavy-rock aficionados, and when TYA attempted to do so by reining in their excesses for a more pop/acoustic direction, even those diehard fans lost interest.

Still, it was good while it lasted – and at least they'd always have Woodstock.

STEPPENWOLF

Some bands are known for one song and one song only. Californian blues rockers Steppenwolf churned out six albums during their initial seven-year career from 1967 to 1972 but will be forever associated with 'Born To Be Wild', the growling, take-no-shit 1968 bikers' anthem that sounded like Jack Kerouac on steroids and even coined a name for the post-Summer of Love dark, menacing bluesy hard rock that was breaking out both in the US and Britain with its lyric: 'heavy metal thunder'.

It was a song that would have sounded far more apposite at Altamont than at Woodstock, an anarchic, lawless, narcotic quest for instant self-gratification. Yet maybe 'Born To Be Wild' came too soon for Steppenwolf: their third single, it became a counter-culture anthem and blasted into mass consciousness after being used in Dennis Hopper's *Easy Rider*. The way was open for them to become major arena-filling players.

They didn't follow through on this promise because they simply didn't have the songs or the nous, although albums *The Second* and *At Your Birthday Party* did okay in the States (although not in the UK: Britain never cared for them) in the wake of their high-profile debut. Singer John Kay had a convincingly macho guttural vocal rasp and their blues riffs took no prisoners, but ultimately Steppenwolf lacked the grace and guile that lifts bands to greatness, leaving them as plucky but limited quasi-metal also-rans.

Now in his early seventies, Kay still occasionally throws together a band, calls them Steppenwolf and chugs around the US nostalgia circuit doing 'Born To Be Wild'. It must be a poignant sight.

Column 7

23 **Ch** **69** Crazy Horse		
24 **Bi** **67** Big Brother & the Holding Company	**28** **Gf** **69** Grand Funk Railroad	**32** **Bs** **70** Black Sabbath
25 **Zt** **71** ZZ Top	**29** **Bo** **72** Blue Öyster Cult	**33** **Vf** **67** Vanilla Fudge
26 **Ty** **67** Ten Years After	**30** **Ab** **69** Allman Brothers Band	**34** **F** **69** Free
27 **S** **68** Steppenwolf	**31** **Ls** **73** Lynyrd Skynrd	**35** **Dp** **68** Deep Purple

GRAND FUNK RAILROAD

Don't allow these Periodic Table classifications to fool you: heavy rock has never been rocket science. That was just as well for Grand Funk Railroad, who sure weren't rocket scientists.

An American institution who meant diddly-squat in Britain and, indeed, most of the rest of the globe, they were a rudimentary bluesy power-trio who achieved their status more by sleeves-rolled-up graft and non-stop touring than by flashes of divine musical inspiration. Formed in Flint, Michigan in 1968 from solid working-class stock, they took their cues slavishly from the likes of the Rolling Stones and Yardbirds and built up a strong following in the Midwest while making lesser impact on the coasts.

You could say what you liked about their lack of originality, and the critics certainly did, but you could certainly never fault Grand Funk Railroad's indefatigable work ethic: despite being rarely off a stage, they chucked out ten studio albums inside their first five years. All but the most diehard fans may have had difficulty telling those albums apart, although in fairness 1972's *Phoenix,* for which they had made the radical move of shortening their name to Grand Funk, did introduce a hint of melody and even the occasional ballad to their usual sludgy sonic swamp.

Yet GFR's defining tune, both philosophically and in terms of it being their sole self-penned US number 1 single, was 1973's 'We're An American Band', a sweaty, charmless slab of boogie metal boasting of life on the road and the number of groupies they had nailed from Little Rock to Omaha. Grand Funk Railroad were an American band, and it was hard not to retort that America was welcome to them.

BLUE ÖYSTER CULT

Blue Öyster Cult may have hoved into view on the hard-rock highway playing urgent, frazzled mutant blues in the style of Steppenwolf or Free, but they were far more literate than those contemporaries, or indeed most others.

Formed while at college in Long Island in the late 1960s, their songs were largely written by their managers, two moonlighting music journalists named Sandy Pearlman and Richard Meltzer, while their three-decade career saw their paths cross with Patti Smith, Stephen King and sci-fi writer (and Hawkwind collaborator) Michael Moorcock.

Yet this relative erudition didn't mean they couldn't rock: their self-named 1972 debut album was knotty, ferocious bluesy psychedelia with gothic lyrical overtones, delivered at a ferocious lick. Two more similarly pulverising albums followed before BÖC shifted tack for 1976's *Agents Of Fortune*, relegating their barroom-boogie-on-amphetamines shtick for a more polished, melodic sound that saw them score their biggest hit with '(Don't Fear) The Reaper', a toe-tapping load of pseudo-mystical hokum that was to become an FM-radio staple.

This triumph proved to be a double-edged sword. Keen to replicate the success of 'Reaper', BÖC became a somewhat schizophrenic entity, trying to hold on to their original biker fans while simultaneously appealing to an MOR audience. Inevitably, in trying to please both sets of followers they satisfied neither, and while they plodded on into the twenty-first century, their last convincing and commercially rewarding album was 1981's *Fire of Unknown Origin*. Thereafter, it was all very much damp squibs for this durable but inessential rock compound.

ALLMAN BROTHERS BAND

Geography and rock and roll should have as little to do with each other as do geography and chemistry, but some facts are just indisputable: the Deep South of

America has never been a hotbed of progressive rock. In their traditionalist yet quietly daring way, the Allman Brothers Band may just be the closest approximation to prog to spring from south of the Mason–Dixon line in the classic rock era, not to mention the fact that their story verged on Shakespearean tragedy.

Formed by guitarist Duane Allman and his vocalist brother Gregg in Georgia in 1969, the Allman Brothers Band tipped country, jazz and soul influences into their chugging, fuzzy deep-fried Southern blues, showing they had a keen ear for the innovations coming out of England via the likes of Jeff Beck and Cream while being conventional and hard-rocking enough to satisfy the local good ol' boys.

It was a balancing act, yet the Allmans were also a visceral, instinctive concern, especially live, where songs would spiral off into freewheeling, impromptu 30-minute improvisational jams that were undeniably heavy but were rarely ponderous.

With their reputation spreading beyond hard-rock circles, the Allman Brothers Band were at a reputational tipping point when Duane Allman was killed in a motorcycle accident. Just over a year later, bassist Berry Oakley died in a second bike smash just a few streets away.

Despite these tragedies, the band's star shone as they enjoyed three platinum albums in the early 1970s, but as Gregg Allman married Cher (twice) and retreated north to Hollywood, and various members attempted solo careers and battled addictions, they naturally foundered then split.

Post-reunion, later years brought mediocre arena rock, then an unexpected creative rebirth, but for most heavy-rock fans the Allman Brothers Band are the group who showed that the Deep South could do more than boogie.

LYNYRD SKYNYRD

Spellcheck-challenging name aside, Lynyrd Skynyrd are certainly among the least complex compounds in hard rock's Periodic Table. Indeed, their heads-down, pathologically single-minded simplicity formed much of their appeal for many 1970s heavy-rock fans, including countless local followers in the Deep South.

(Mis-)named after a disliked local high-school teacher, a certain Leonard Skinner, Skynyrd took the prog-rock boogie of contemporaries the Allman Brothers and dumbed it down to its bones. They may have been heavy in volume and riffing, but their rough, functional amalgamation of blues, country and hard-edged rock was essentially an aural definition of the phrase 'no-nonsense'.

Lynyrd Skynyrd were never likely to attract an art-rock or hip metropolitan following, but their defiant lack of frills gained them a loyal army of Confederate flag-waving, denim-clad acolytes, who thrilled to the stripped-down workouts of their self-named 1973 debut album (subtitled 'Pronounced Leh-nerd Skin-nerd', for the slower members of the class). Its standout track, 'Free Bird', remains a classic-rock FM-radio staple to this day.

Yet if Skynyrd were viewed as sweaty, undistinguished hard rock, it wasn't for any lack of intelligence: their chief songwriter and singer Ronnie Van Zant was capable, when he chose, of sprinkling fiendishly clever, idiosyncratic twists into their chugging mix. Even so, Skynyrd became indelibly etched into music history as incorrigible rednecks when they penned the anthemic 'Sweet Home Alabama', stoutly defending the good-ol'-boy lifestyle against the perceived slight that was Neil Young's 'Southern Man'.

Ironically, this most prosaic of rock bands gained a romantic, mythic sheen in October 1977 when their chartered flight from South Carolina to Louisiana suffered engine problems and crashed in woodland in Mississippi, killing Van Zant and guitarist Steve Gaines outright.

Ferrous Metals

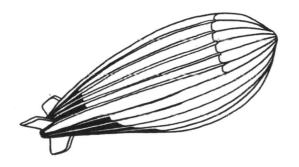

For our purposes, 'ferrous metal' defines the bands who wrought such wanton damage upon their source material of the blues that they spawned its most bastardised, revered and reviled form: heavy metal.

History has pinned Black Sabbath as the genre's originators: for their lugubrious sludge metal, they famously drew upon the brutal noises of the engineering factories in which they had laboured in their native Birmingham.

Iron is not the only ferrous metal. Leavening their own din with blues and soul, Led Zeppelin were assuredly heavy rock's steel; Jeff Beck's sleek, metallic virtuosity shone as bright as stainless steel; once they were shorn of their early pretensions, the strong yet brittle riffing of Deep Purple suggested cast iron.

To aesthetes and metal non-devotees, the ferrous metallers are not the most beauteous music: the grunting Bad Company were aural pig iron. This was disenchanted, disgruntled, outsider music – and as heavy metal, it was to seduce and thrill millions.

Column 8

28 **Gf** 69 Grand Funk Railroad	32 **Bs** 70 Black Sabbath	36 **Lz** 69 Led Zeppelin
29 **Bo** 72 Blue Öyster Cult	33 **Vf** 67 Vanilla Fudge	37 **Y** 65 Yardbirds
30 **Ab** 69 Allman Brothers Band	34 **F** 69 Free	38 **Jb** 68 Jeff Beck Group
31 **Ls** 73 Lynyrd Skynrd	35 **Dp** 68 Deep Purple	39 **Bd** 74 Bad Company

BLACK SABBATH

32	70
Bs	
Black Sabbath	

Many are the bands who have been credited with inventing heavy metal, but undoubtedly that crown belongs firmly on the head of Black Sabbath.

Before the legendary Birmingham band came along, even the most primal hard rock still bore some relation to the blues. Sabbath took the hope and faith in adversity that has always been the bedrock of blues and replaced it with angst, despair and nihilism.

There was an element of luck to the manner in which they arrived at their uniquely bleak image and music: they nicked their name from a film playing at their local pictures, and their funereal sound was largely a result of guitarist Tony Iommi losing two fingertips in an industrial accident, thus reducing his musical versatility.

Yet once they chanced across their formula, the results were astonishing. Their second album, 1970's *Paranoid*, reached number 1 in Britain despite – or due to – being composed of doleful, skull- and soul-crushing dirges about war, death and depression.

It was clear to anybody that Sabbath had severe limitations: the first lines of the album's apocalyptic Book of Revelations-style opener, 'War Pigs', rhymed 'masses' with 'masses', and Ozzy Osbourne's vocal was a needling Brummie whine. Yet somehow these very restrictions emphasised the mood of suffocating frustration Sabbath were articulating.

Their next three classic metal sacred texts, *Master Of Reality, Black Sabbath. Vol. 4* and *Sabbath Bloody Sabbath* hit a similarly doom-laden (minor) chord, but after Osbourne left the band, it became largely the Tony Iommi show, with a string of replacement vocalists including Ronnie James Dio, Ian Gillan and Glenn Hughes all failing to replicate Osbourne's flawed and yet compelling magic.

How crucial in the development of heavy rock were Black Sabbath? Every one of the bands in the base-metals section of this Periodic Table will view them with the veneration that pop bands show to the Beatles.

33		67
	Vf	
	Vanilla	
	Fudge	

VANILLA FUDGE

Initially, Vanilla Fudge appeared not to be a rock chemical entity in their own right, but an alloy of already existing elements and styles. Why? Because they took other bands' songs and they duffed them up.

The Fudge emerged in 1967 with a version of Diana Ross and the Supremes' 'You Keep Me Hangin' On' that eviscerated the original. The dainty dynamics of the Holland-Dozier-Holland soul number were crushed beneath swathes of swampy psychedelia, titanic drumming and the guttural howl of singer Mark Stein.

Nor was it a one-off: as this grisly musical mugging rocketed up the Billboard chart, Vanilla Fudge followed it up with a whole album of similarly sludgy, hypnotic re-imaginings of pop classics by artists including Curtis Mayfield, the Beatles and even Cher.

These offerings thoroughly polarised the music lovers of the Summer of Love. Some critics descried Vanilla Fudge as one-trick ponies unable to produce their own original material, while others lauded them for giving seemingly superficial chart-pop fodder unsuspected levels of import and meaning.

Yet they were hugely influential: Yes founder Jon Anderson called them his teenage musical eureka moment, while Deep Purple adopted them as a template. When Vanilla Fudge toured the US at the height of their fame, their management (bizarrely, fully made Mafia men) told them to take along as their support an upcoming young British band named Led Zeppelin, whose drummer, John Bonham, nicked Fudge drummer Carmine Appice's tricks and sleights-of-hand wholesale.

Sadly, Vanilla Fudge's reputation was dealt a deadly blow by their second album, a preposterous concept record named *The Beat Goes On* that featured thirteenth-century death marches, snatches of Mozart and Beethoven, and Hitler addressing a Nuremberg rally. Even for the anything-goes rock 1960s, *that* was a step too far.

FREE

As 1970s as flared trousers, lava lamps and three-day weeks, Free were an archetypal British hard-rock band who melded the blues, heavy metal and rock and roll into an unashamed, raucous quest for a good time.

They came together in the late 1960s and hit the ground running, releasing two under-performing albums of nearly all self-composed songs at a time when most new bands were still sticking out covers of blues greats.

Vocalist Paul Rodgers and guitarist Paul Kossoff clearly had a rough-and-ready chemistry, but they really hit their stride as the 1970s dawned with 'All Right Now', a lewd, lecherous and carnal slug of the blues-metal hard stuff that crossed over from hardcore rock fans to the mainstream, hitting number 1 in 20 countries and going top 5 in Britain and America.

As with Steppenwolf and 'Born To Be Wild', 'All Right Now' immediately turned into Free's anthem, theme tune and millstone, and much like their US counterparts, they failed to capitalise on the opportunity it yielded them, instead releasing a surprisingly mellow and low-key album in *Highway* and then splitting, weary of life on the road and of each other.

Yet various solo projects were ignominious failures and in little more than a year Free were back, reverting to hard-rocking mutant-blues type on the *Free At Last* album. It was only a minor hit and at the same time Kossoff's long-term drug habit was taking its toll, with the guitarist scarcely able to play, let along write, on their final album, 1973's *Heartbreaker*.

This career coda did at least spawn the second stone-cold classic of their career in the yearning, muscular 'Wishing Well', Rodgers's fond adieu to the fading Kossoff, who was to OD just three years later. Rodgers went on to form a group whose chemical formula was even more basic than Free's: Bad Company.

35   68

Dp

Deep Purple

DEEP PURPLE

There are many kinds of heavy rock and Deep Purple have played most of them. Having in their early years become a byword for self-regarding, over-reaching progressive rock, they went on to morph into lumbering heavy metallers and a stepping-stone for some of the biggest names in this table's base-metals section.

These included Ritchie Blackmore and Ian Gillan, who were present and incorrect in 1970 when the earnest Purple, fixated on melding rock and classical music, teamed up with the Royal Philharmonic Orchestra to record the much-mocked *Concerto For Group And Orchestra*.

Stung by this setback, they quickly abandoned some of their loftier aesthetic ambitions, transformed into full-on head-bangers and dialled up the decibels. The *Deep Purple In Rock* album, which was released later in 1970, pretty much spelled out their revised agenda and their gigs soon became all about dandruff and denim, while studio sessions yielded a slew of deafening but dexterous albums of which the apex was 1972's multi-platinum *Machine Head* with its timeless lead single, 'Smoke On The Water'.

There were so many competing egos in Deep Purple that there was bound to be a cost, and in 1974 Blackmore and Gillan left to form Rainbow and, er, Gillan respectively, while a caterwauling newcomer named David Coverdale took over on vocals. The band split then re-formed its most popular line-up, although alarums and excursions followed as Gillan and Blackmore seemingly took turns in re-joining then re-quitting the group.

A resilient chemical compound, Deep Purple resurface sporadically even today, yet their defining legacy remains that every rock guitarist in this Periodic Table will, at some point in their adolescent years, have sat hunched over a Fender or a Gibson to master 'Smoke On The Water'.

Column 9

32 **70** **Bs** Black Sabbath	**36** **69** **Lz** Led Zeppelin	**40** **67** **Jh** Jimi Hendrix Experience
33 **67** **Vf** Vanilla Fudge	**37** **65** **Y** Yardbirds	**41** **64** **Rs** Rolling Stones
34 **69** **F** Free	**38** **68** **Jb** Jeff Beck Group	**42** **63** **B** Beatles
35 **68** **Dp** Deep Purple	**39** **74** **Bd** Bad Company	**43** **66** **Cm** Cream

36		69
	Lz	
Led Zeppelin		

LED ZEPPELIN

There is a persuasive argument that Led Zeppelin, even today, remain the heaviest element in rock's Periodic Table.

Their gravity and gravitas was rooted not just in speed, riffs and volume (because any one can do that) but in lyrical and spiritual portentousness. Inspired to varying degrees by Delta blues, rock and roll and Celtic folk, Zeppelin took these mongrel influences and transformed them into something mythic, monolithic and majestic.

They are frequently credited as progenitors of heavy metal, but there was always more to Zeppelin's rock maelstrom than Jimmy Page's seismic, primeval riffs. Even on their eponymous 1968 debut album, tracks like 'Dazed And Confused' showed they were capable of crafting bludgeoning, labyrinthine rock ruminations with a thrilling lightness of touch.

Amid Page's steel-wristed riffing and the near-certifiable John Bonham's wild-man drumming, Robert Plant's raucous, possessed howl suggested that he had met Robert Johnson's devil at the crossing and gone ahead and sealed the deal.

Zeppelin's base elements were often discernible – Hendrix's white-noise screes; Cream's rambling psychedelia – but they were always so much more than the sum of their parts. They were also enchantingly, audaciously preposterous, with Plant producing a steady stream of cod-mystical lyrical reveries apparently intent on decoding the meaning of life itself.

Ridicule, Zeppelin clearly figured, was nothing to be scared of. Instead of mockery they attracted adulation, with millions of fans across the globe buying into this most inscrutable of groups.

Their commercial high-water mark, the gnomic epic 'Stairway To Heaven', regularly tops polls of the Greatest Rock Song Ever, even if its cryptic, gale-force-gibberish narrative of bustles in hedgerows and spring-cleaning May Queens remains utterly impenetrable. Some of their members grew notorious for their chemical excesses, but it was Zeppelin's indelible rock alchemy that burned hardest and brightest.

YARDBIRDS

It's tempting to view the Yardbirds as a hard-rock academy. At their 1960s peak, no fewer than three iconic guitar heroes graduated from this ballsy, frequently experimental heavy-blues band, although the success that the group enjoyed was never proportionate to their talent.

Originally a covers group reproducing old Delta blues standards on the same London circuit as early 1960s contemporaries the Rolling Stones, the Yardbirds's trump card was the prodigious guitar playing of the teenage Eric Clapton. Even at 18, Clapton was a purist, and when the band scored a big 1964 British and American hit with 'For Your Love', a song written by future 10cc man Graham Gouldman, which Clapton considered lightweight pop fodder, he left in disgust.

His replacement was a then-unknown Jeff Beck, who added layers of experimentation, exoticism and psychedelic excess to the Yardbirds's twisted blues. Despite uneven material – none of their number was a great songwriter – the band scored occasional hits, and their virtuosity underwent a further quantum leap in 1966 when Jimmy Page joined them, initially on bass and then as a joint lead guitarist. Even 50 years on, fans would salivate at the prospect of a Page and Beck forward line, but the pairing lasted only weeks before the reliably erratic Beck quit the band, citing fatigue.

Even the band's formidable heaviness then bit the dust, as they oddly teamed up with producer and pop impresario Mickie Most, who targeted them firmly at the charts. He had modest success with faux-psychedelic cuts like 'Ha Ha Said The Clown' but the Yardbirds had lost their direction and their balls, and split in 1968.

That could have been that... had Page not formed the New Yardbirds, who quickly morphed into the rather better known Led Zeppelin.

38		68
	Jb	
	Jeff Beck Group	

JEFF BECK GROUP

It is unlikely that this Periodic Table possesses a more rogue element than the gifted but seemingly randomly ricocheting genius that is Jeff Beck.

Beck has been widely acknowledged as a bona fide guitar hero in hard-rock circles since the 1960s. There have been so many times that the music world has appeared to be his for the taking, only for him to pull one of his trademark odd reverse manoeuvres, turn down a career cul-de-sac or simply vanish into thin air.

Beck's extraordinary virtuosity and knack for recalibrating heavy rock was noted as soon as he replaced Eric Clapton in the Yardbirds in 1964 but he responded to this acclaim by 'retiring' two years later. On his return in 1967 he formed the Jeff Beck Group with Rod Stewart and Ronnie Wood and specialised in riff-frenzied muggings of old blues classics and Elvis songs: to all intents and purposes, it was heavy metal before heavy metal was invented, but it didn't score remotely the success that Stewart and Wood were to enjoy in the Faces.

Beck's next move was to wrench the volume up in Beck, Bogert & Appice, a power-rock trio with the rhythm section from Vanilla Fudge, before he unexpectedly diversified into jazz fusion in the mid-1970s, recorded with Nile Rodgers, played guitar on solo albums by Mick Jagger and Roger Waters, and released a tribute to Gene Vincent.

Even in 2010 (yet) another Beck comeback album, *Emotion & Commotion*, won acclaim and a pair of Grammies, yet Jeff Beck's pinball-table career remains the story of one of hard rock's truly prodigious talents lacking the focus, staying power or attention span fully to exploit his genius.

Sadly, however, the theory that he formed the template for gifted-but-dim guitar wizard Nigel Tufnel in *This Is Spinal Tap* is almost certainly apocryphal.

39	74
Bd	
Bad Company	

BAD COMPANY

Archetypal 1970s blues-metal sloggers Bad Company were somewhat disingenuously named, as in hard-rock terms they were extremely well connected. A raucous supergroup formed of former Free vocalist Paul Rodgers and drummer Simon Kirke, Mott the Hoople guitar player Mick Ralphs and King Crimson bassist Boz Burrell, they were also the first signings to Led Zeppelin's Swan Song record label.

Given this reputational cocktail, it is probably no surprise that their 1974 debut album – powered by the hit single 'Can't Get Enough' – went to the top of the US chart, yet in truth Bad Company were an elementary compound with few exceptional qualities.

Having helped to craft King Crimson's abstract arabesques, it is hard to imagine exactly what Burrell got out of holding down Bad Company's meat-and-potatoes bluesy workouts, which left even the reductive Free sounding like the music of the spheres by comparison.

Yet even if Bad Company played it by the hoary old hard-rock book, they were experienced lags who knew their way around a fretboard, a studio and a stage, meaning they were able to squeeze out sporadic pop-metal crossover hits such as 'Good Lovin' Gone Bad' and 'Feel Like Makin' Love', then muster the elbow grease to churn 'em out live with crowd-pleasing volume, energy and efficiency.

They were monolithic, macho and smelled of denim, beer and tour-bus exhaust fuel, but that is how some people (particularly in America) like their heavy rock, and Bad Company carried on head-down riffing until the 1980s, when they found that people's tastes had moved on and their appeal was suddenly decidedly more selective.

Complex Metals

Heavy rock can anchor itself in the sublime or the ridiculous, and all points in-between. As the ferrous metallers looked to reduce the form down to its elemental core, others strove to elevate rock and roll to the pantheon of high art.

Few would see those joint 1960s pop talismans the Beatles and the Rolling Stones as quintessential heavy rockers, but their more outré excursions into psychedelic pop expanded its power and parameters.

Before his tragic death, Jimi Hendrix relocated the electric guitar on a whole new astral plane. Likewise, the Who, the Doors and Cream stayed plugged into rock and roll's power grid, while crafting music of vast intelligence and ambition.

It was only the beginning. In the wake of the pioneering Pink Floyd came a whole swathe of progressive rock artists who looked to imbue rock with the import of theatre, literature and poetry. Emerson, Lake & Palmer composed a classical symphony for an orchestra; Yes recounted *Tales From Topographic Oceans*.

Heavy rock was no longer wearing its brusque simplicity as a badge of honour. In an anything-goes musical era of exploration and experimentation, here suddenly were the most complex of metals.

Column 10

36 **69** **Lz** Led Zeppelin	**40** **67** **Jh** Jimi Hendrix Experience	**44** **65** **W** Who
37 **65** **Y** Yardbirds	**41** **64** **Rs** Rolling Stones	**45** **66** **D** Doors
38 **68** **Jb** Jeff Beck Group	**42** **63** **B** Beatles	**46** **67** **Pf** Pink Floyd
39 **74** **Bd** Bad Company	**43** **66** **Cm** Cream	**47** **70** **Ha** Hawkwind

40		67
	Jh	
	Jimi Hendrix	
	Experience	

JIMI HENDRIX EXPERIENCE

Jimi Hendrix was not so much an element in a Periodic Table of heavy rock as an entire elemental spectrum in a parallel universe. More than anybody else in hard-rock history, he sought to take rock to a different place, to free it from its earthly moorings, to fire it with limitless imagination, to transcend.

A keen student of music, Hendrix was hyper-aware of what his peers were doing, and yet the celestial ejaculations he would routinely coax from his fretboard would effortlessly surpass them. Put simply, he was in love with the guitar, the instrument that he would carry with him 24/7 in his youth and even in his woefully misguided spell in the US Army.

Initially, his influences were routine ones – Memphis Blues, Elvis, he even spent a time in Little Richard's band – but when he formed his own group, the Jimi Hendrix Experience, he set the controls for another cosmos entirely.

Uniquely, Hendrix discovered whole new galaxies of sound within six strings, patented a fresh lexicon in which to speak in tongues: his ground-breaking embrace of feedback, and his theatrical flourishes of playing his guitar behind his back and with his teeth before setting fire to it, all spoke of his frustrations with the physical limitations of the instrument.

Hendrix's genius was so ferocious that he regularly reduced his peers to stunned silence. Paul McCartney described hearing him play 'Sgt. Pepper's Lonely Hearts Club Band' as the greatest honour imaginable, while Eric Clapton admitted that after hearing Hendrix, 'My life was never the same.' Hendrix's combustible, inflammatory – in every sense of the words – rendition of 'The Star Spangled Banner' at Woodstock remains a miracle not just of art but of science and nature: *How did he do that?*

There was nothing base about Jimi Hendrix: he was rock's purest element.

41   64
Rs
Rolling
Stones

ROLLING STONES

Forget about the pensionable-age, grotesque travelling circus nowadays ridiculed as the Strolling Bones and gaze instead at the flickering monochrome footage of when the Rolling Stones were a vital, life-affirming, society-changing rock-and-roll band.

Having began life in 1962 in thrall to America's Delta bluesmen and first-generation rock and rollers, the Stones hit on their own identity when they started writing their own songs and augmenting attitudinal blues rhythms with a malevolent, snarling edge.

It naturally helped that their strutting, simian singer Mick Jagger and insouciant cigarette-masticating guitarist Keith Richards were superb showmen, and abrasive mid-1960s hit singles like '(I Can't Get No) Satisfaction' and '19th Nervous Breakdown', plus an adroit PR campaign painting them as fearful rock outlaws, cemented their superstar status.

The Stones's unexpected left-turn into the 1967 psychedelic concept album *Their Satanic Majesties Request* never truly convinced, and felt as if they merely felt pressured to compete with their arch-rivals the Beatles and *Sgt. Pepper's Lonely Hearts Club Band*, but when the Stones jettisoned the dark whimsy and returned to the raunch and roll that was their lifeblood, they hit a stupendous run of form with records such as *Beggars Banquet* and 1972 double album *Exile On Main Street*.

Once they hit the 1980s their creative well ran dry and they morphed into essentially a global stadium-touring nostalgia treat for baby boomers; an avaricious money-raking franchise behind that appropriate logo of two juicy, leering lips.

Yet as acolytes from Iggy Pop to the Faces to Aerosmith to New York Dolls would concur, when the Jagger/Richards chemistry was firing at its peak, the Rolling Stones may even have deserved the sobriquet they cockily awarded themselves: the World's Greatest Rock and Roll Band.

42		63
	B	
	Beatles	

BEATLES

It's fitting that the Beatles sit at the heart of this Periodic Table as their tentacles reach into the weave of every genre of modern pop music – heavy rock included.

They may have begun as purveyors of skiffle and frantic teen pop but as their stature and celebrity grew, they did the exact opposite of selling out by focusing ever deeper on their art – even abandoning touring to give themselves more time in the studio. In 1967 alone they recorded not one but two concept albums in the brilliantly eclectic and visionary *Sgt. Pepper's Lonely Heart's Club Band,* and the valiant if flawed soundtrack to the *Magical Mystery Tour* movie.

Pop came so easy to Lennon and McCartney that at times it bored them, which was why they ventured deep into the more outré realms of psychedelic excess and also genuine titanium-edged heavy rock. Their 1968 double album *The Beatles,* or the *White Album* as it is usually known, featured both the pitch-black freak-out of 'Helter Skelter' (which Charles Manson was to famously claim as inspiration for his warped Hollywood massacre) and the we're-doing-this-because-we-can headfuck sonic collage 'Revolution 9'.

The Beatles were the biggest, best and most important band in music history not just because of Lennon/McCartney's almost illegally felicitous way with melodies and choruses, but due to their innate, insatiable boundary-pushing sense of curiosity. By the end of their scarcely believable career, as they surrendered to bile and intra-band tension, even their supposedly bubblegum singles such as 'Get Back' and 'Come Together' were acerbic, pitch-black essays in pop noir.

The greatest compliment of all: the Beatles' influence extends into every box on this Periodic Table. And if any band denies that, they are lying.

43	66
Cm	
Cream	

CREAM

A cynic might suggest that the heaviest elements of Cream were the band members' egos.

When former Yardbirds and John Mayall & The Bluesbreakers guitarist Eric Clapton teamed up with bassist/singer Jack Bruce and drummer Ginger Baker in 1966, their undoubted rarefied musicality was equalled only by their lofty self-esteem. Their broad mission statement was to bring some of the improvisational capacity of free jazz to bluesy rock, even though their debut album, *Fresh Cream*, was largely traditional R&B given plenty of welly.

Thereafter, however, Cream moved into more experimental and ground-breaking terrain, infiltrating dark-tinged melodic pop and sinister psychedelic tropes into the maw of their belligerent blues. Typical was malevolent 1967 single 'Sunshine Of Your Love', a huge hit in America, which made a pledge of love sound like a brooding threat.

Heavier than, say, the Rolling Stones yet with impressive pop smarts, Cream capitalised on their US status when their 1968 double album, *Wheels On Fire*, became number 1 there, and yet Clapton & Co viewed hard rock as an expansive medium. Indeed, they often ladled out too much of a good thing, with many of their relatively succinct album tracks stretched out to tediously noodling ten-minute bluesy jams when they played live.

Yet Cream pulled off a rare balancing act of melding thrilling, menacingly dystopian soundscapes and canny chart-friendly melodies, and they were bestriding the rock landscape towards the end of 1968 when... they split.

With hindsight, it was no surprise, and nor was the demise of the Clapton–Baker supergroup, Blind Faith, that followed. Clapton's ever-ballooning ego and crass need to be a bona fide guitar god precluded sharing his limelight with anyone at all, while the ornery, truculent Baker went on to spend the next 30 years proving himself the most unpleasant man in rock.

Column 11

40 Jh 67 Jimi Hendrix Experience	44 W 65 Who	48 Ru 74 Rush
41 Rs 64 Rolling Stones	45 D 66 Doors	49 Ib 68 Iron Butterfly
42 B 63 Beatles	46 Pf 67 Pink Floyd	50 Gd 67 Grateful Dead
43 Cm 66 Cream	47 Ha 70 Hawkwind	51 Vg 69 Van der Graaf Generator

44		65
	W	
	Who	

WHO

Some elements in rock's chemical table are easily defined, their properties straightforward ones. The Who are an alloy that defy easy categorisation.

This most singular of groups, most British of bands, began life in London in the mid-1960s as routine rockers influenced by American blues and soul, even defining their output as 'Maximum R&B'. After a flirtation with the Mod scene, they discovered they had two unique selling points in their arsenal: guitarist Pete Townshend's acute songwriting skills, and a propensity towards wanton violence that saw Townshend and their frenzied drummer Keith Moon frequently destroy their instruments onstage.

Early singles were indebted to the observational London pop of the Kinks, but as Townshend produced a string of barbed, bitter gems such as 'My Generation' and 'Substitute', a visceral anger burned through the Who's serrated rock. They were an energy jolt, a short, sharp shock of a band, yet they had more strings to their bow: gaining in confidence and experience, Townshend was to write serious narrative-driven rock-opera concept albums, in *Tommy* and *Quadrophenia*, that were as ambitious and audacious as any progressive rock.

By the early 1970s, their rare fusion of imagination, danger, showmanship and propulsive hard rock arguably made the Who the second-biggest live draw in the world after the Rolling Stones. Yet where the Stones were settling into being a slick, crowd-pleasing greatest-hits machine, the Who were perennially tense and conflicted, its members constantly battling substance abuse and each other. It's telling that the troubled Townshend foresaw the birth of punk as heralding the death of the Who when the Sex Pistols, for one, loved their rage and energy.

The two surviving members, Townshend and singer Roger Daltrey, sporadically tour the world's arenas, but more important is the Who's high-octane legacy. Few compounds in this table are as explosive.

DOORS

Were he required to state his artistic influences, the indefatigably pretentious Jim Morrison would be unlikely to quote the Rolling Stones or Van Morrison, although he and his band were undeniably beholden to both. Instead, he would be more likely to produce a roll call of writers and philosophers: Nietzsche, Plutarch, Rimbaud, Kerouac and Cocteau.

Taking their name from Aldous Huxley's *The Doors of Perception* – itself a steal from literature's very first psychedelic rock god, William Blake – the Doors from the outset appeared to view themselves more as poetic shamen than as mere musicians. Yet in many ways, Jim Morrison was rock and roll incarnate. A strutting, transgressive vision in leather trousers and a major fuck-you attitude, the man also known as the Lizard King and the (anagrammatic) Mr Mojo Risin' was a huge influence on wide-eyed acolytes such as Iggy Pop, Alice Cooper and Julian Casablancas. 'I knew Jim Morrison,' Cooper once told me, 'and when he died, aged 27, I wasn't surprised: I was just surprised that he had lived that long.'

While the Doors's musical staple was mildly psychedelic blues, Morrison's taboo-shaking lyrical preoccupations, messianic posturing and relentless pursuit of alcoholic and narcotic oblivion made him a beacon of late-sixties US counter-culture. He was on a perpetual driven, erratic quest for profundity, whether improvising whisky-fuelled freeform poetry between songs, attempting a lurid dissection of man's Oedipal urges in 'The End', or, more bathetically, getting arrested for exposing himself onstage.

Ultimately, the Doors were as celebrated for their lyrical cosmic meanderings as for their often-workaday music, although one dissident school of thought still holds that the deepest thing about Jim Morrison was the bath water in which he drowned in Paris.

46		67
	Pf	
	Pink Floyd	

PINK FLOYD

It's ironic that Pink Floyd took their name from a pair of Piedmont bluesmen, splicing together the monikers of Pink Anderson and Floyd Council, as their own output could hardly be less grounded in ragtime rhythms.

These colossi of heavy rock began as purveyors of quixotic, wondrous acid pop shaped by singer and guitarist Syd Barrett until Barrett's acid-induced mental illness led him to quit the band, leaving bassist Roger Waters at the helm, at which point they morphed into a different entity entirely.

Throughout the 1970s, Pink Floyd turned out a majestic sequence of immaculate visionary records and concept pieces that acknowledged hard rock, folk and space pop and yet sounded like beautifully atmospheric, textured telegrams from a better future.

This purple patch reached its zenith in 1973's colossal *Dark Side Of The Moon*, the sumptuous symphony which became a compulsory purchase for every greatcoat-clad, patchouli-scented 1970s student and has sold a staggering 50 million copies to date.

When Waters quit the band in 1983, guitarist David Gilmour took Pink Floyd in a statelier, more chillaxed direction, but by then their legacy was assured. During their stellar career, they exploded the myth that ambitious heavy rock could not penetrate beyond culture's margins, as well as inadvertently helping to shape musical genres as various as overblown 1980s US arena rock (which it would be harsh to blame them for) and pre- and post-millennium ambient electro.

More than just a precious element in this table, Pink Floyd were a heavy-rock catalyst.

47		70
	Ha	
	Hawkwind	

HAWKWIND

Few heavy rockers have succeeded in uniting hippies, Hells Angels, punks and New Age thinkers alike in approbation, but Hawkwind are among their number.

Defying all natural laws of physics, biology and chemistry, this renegade band has for well over four decades been whipping up a brooding, dark psychedelic churn of renegade rock that may well be precisely where the Beatles meet heavy metal.

Their veteran leader and guitarist Dave Brock formed the band in London in 1969, just as Altamont and Charles Manson were bringing down an axe upon the neck of the flower-power generation across the Atlantic. His declared intention was to make music that 'recreated the sensation of an acid trip' and he didn't stint on the first-hand research.

Underground-press writer Robert Calvert joined to sing space-rock odysseys such as 'Master Of The Universe' as sci-fi author Michael Moorcock helped Hawkwind, by now with future Motörhead singer Lemmy in their ranks, conceptualise their 1972 *Space Ritual* tour, complete with dancers, mime artists and a lighting plan predicated on the colours of the spheres.

Hawkwind could only have been bigger societal outsiders if they had had the word 'Freaks' tattooed on their foreheads, yet in 1972 they had an unexpected brush with the mainstream when a thrumming spiral of hard rock called 'Silver Machine' – sung by Lemmy – hit number 3 on the UK singles chart.

Their outlaw, band-of-the-people status meant they escaped the disdain showered by punks on the more well-heeled, plummy prog rockers such as Pink Floyd and, despite the countless line-up changes that have seen more than 50 people pass through their ranks, Hawkwind are now closing in on their own half-century. And they *still* sound like an acid trip.

Column 12

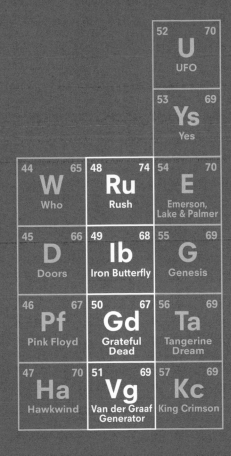

52	70
U	
UFO	

53	69
Ys	
Yes	

44	65
W	
Who	

48	74
Ru	
Rush	

54	70
E	
Emerson, Lake & Palmer	

45	66
D	
Doors	

49	68
Ib	
Iron Butterfly	

55	69
G	
Genesis	

46	67
Pf	
Pink Floyd	

50	67
Gd	
Grateful Dead	

56	69
Ta	
Tangerine Dream	

47	70
Ha	
Hawkwind	

51	69
Vg	
Van der Graaf Generator	

57	69
Kc	
King Crimson	

RUSH

Since the 1970s, generally speaking, hard rock has rarely been hip. The modern hipsters' tastes are for music that is more spectral, ethereal, rarefied. On the few occasions in the last four decades when heavy rock *has* been in vogue, it has been of an arty or political bent – a Jane's Addiction or a Rage Against the Machine. Few bands, though, have ever been quite so terminally unhip as Rush.

Formed in Canada in 1968 as a heavy-rock trio indebted to the likes of Cream and Vanilla Fudge, Rush came into their own in 1976 with their fourth album, *2112*, an unholy fusion of dystopian science fiction, complex riffing and the acquired-taste high-pitched trill of singer Geddy Lee. The melodramatic, histrionic narrative about an intergalactic war won by the fascistic 'Red Star of the Solar Federation' who promptly ban rock and roll was irredeemably silly, but appealed to teenage geeks the world over (and was also hugely influential, to say the least, on both Styx's *Kilroy Was Here* album and, decades later, Ben Elton's *We Will Rock You* Queen musical).

2112 established the template for a heavy-rock career that would see Rush tip out a succession of ambitious but wincingly clunky albums universally derided by the cognoscenti yet loved by their diehard sci-fi-loving perpetual-adolescent fanbase who invariably fired them to platinum status.

Critical credibility and kudos eluded Rush, but they formed a bridge from the conceptualising prog rockers of the 1970s to the slick arena-pleasers of the following decade – and they sold 40 million albums while doing so. Far out!

IRON BUTTERFLY

They were named Iron Butterfly. Their first album was called *Heavy*. These Californian psychedelic sludge rockers were very much of their time, dating from a ponderous era when bands wore their musical and psychological heft and gravitas like a badge of honour.

They got their first breaks supporting the Doors, possibly picking up their sense of audacious expansiveness, as well as Jefferson Airplane, but when their 1968 debut appeared, it was big on lumpen, cack-handed guitar riffs and drums like seismic tremors, but notably short on tunes.

After the album came out to fairly universal indifference, Iron Butterfly reshuffled their line-up and put out a second album, *In-A-Gadda-Da-Vida*. This was a far superior document, but it was distinguished and dwarfed by its closing, and title, track, a 17-minute droning excursion into frazzled acid rock which performed numerous baked circuits of its looped, distorted guitars, blinkered drumming and random organ parps.

If you wanted to get into it, you had to be out of it, and legend had it that the blissed-out Butterfly had been so stoned when they recorded the track that they had simply banged on, unable to enunciate the lyrics properly and incapable of getting off the cosmic ride. Whatever its genesis, 'In-A-Gadda-Da-Vida' was a tokers' delight, an immersive joy and absolute zenith/nadir (delete according to taste) of a certain strain of take-no-prisoners quasi-metal psychedelia.

Once they sobered up, they were never able to top this crowning glory: *Ball*, their third album, attempted to widen their musical palate and even included a few melodies and tunes, but simply wasn't as hypnotic and alluring, and Iron Butterfly came to the end of their life cycle. They may have been ferrous, or even feral, but they lacked quicksilver.

GRATEFUL DEAD

It's not just rock and metal that can be heavy. So can folk, country and even bluegrass music, if played with intensity, integrity and a gloriously offhand, anti-establishment disdain for narrow conventionality. In mid-1960s California, the Grateful Dead didn't so much embody the counter-culture as virtually invent it.

A shifting collective founded around the hard-partying yet deeply idealistic singer-songwriter Jerry Garcia, they began (initially as the Warlocks) as the house band at Ken Kesey's infamous Acid Test LSD parties as well as playing scores of free hippy parties around San Francisco. They were a trip in every way, with their lengthy, no-curfew live sets generally being impromptu jams incorporating psychedelia, garage rock and their own improvisational take on the blues.

They were also the freewheeling soundtrack to countless scenes of Summer of Love narcotic and sexual debauchery, and there is no doubt that to horrified Middle America, the Grateful Dead appeared so heavy and wanton that they verged on the satanic, even if their music was often relatively light and capricious.

By now supported by a vast tie-dyed army of acid-gobbling devoted followers known as the Deadheads, the Dead initially failed to transfer the epic, sprawling freak-out of their live happenings to record, a situation they rectified by putting out live albums such as 1969's *Live/Dead*, including the 20-minute-plus meandering 'Dark Star'. In the 1970s a few of their less wild-eyed, more accessible offerings even found favour on FM radio but the Dead's instincts remained impeccably transgressive.

Prog rock's ultimate outlaws rolled on through the decades as various band members fell to substance issues, but when Garcia himself died of a heart attack at a rehab facility in 1985, the self-defined 'long, strange trip' was finally over.

VAN DER GRAAF GENERATOR

Any good physicist knows that every action has an equal and opposite reaction, and it was entirely understandable that many prog rockers of the late 1960s and early 1970s reacted against the sunny,

Summer-of-Love positivity of the hippy bands who had preceded them. Yet few of the weightier prog merchants manifested a more doom-laden, existential air of menace than Van der Graaf Generator.

Essentially a vehicle for singer/songwriter/multi-instrumentalist Peter Hammill, Van der Graaf's portentous prognostications hung around Hugh Banton's preternaturally brooding keyboard runs, some seriously off-kilter guitars and drums, and Hammill's own uniquely eerie and accusatory rasped and histrionic vocals (indeed, one young tyro may have been paying very close attention: in 1977 Johnny Rotten, a long-time VDGG fan, opined that 'David Bowie copped a lot from Hammill', and he was probably right).

Like any true prog rocker, Hammill was big on mysticism and obscurantism, having little truck with anything as vulgar as melodies or choruses and delighting in giving his abstruse albums titles such as *The Least We Can Do Is Wave To Each Other* and 1970's *H To He Who Am The Only One*. The latter, much admired by many of the artier post-punks who would happen along a decade later, featured the atypically melodious eight-minute odyssey 'Killer', which was as near as VDGG got to acknowledging the existence of mere pop music.

After Van der Graaf Generator split (i.e., Hammill decided he'd had enough) in the late 1970s, they left behind a striking but under-appreciated legacy: they may never have been big, but they were certainly clever.

Column 13

52 **70** **U** UFO	**58** **75** **J** Journey
53 **69** **Ys** Yes	**59** **77** **Fr** Foreigner

48 **74** **Ru** Rush	**54** **70** **E** Emerson, Lake & Palmer	**60** **71** **Ro** REO Speedwagon
49 **68** **Ib** Iron Butterfly	**55** **69** **G** Genesis	**61** **76** **Bt** Boston
50 **67** **Gd** Grateful Dead	**56** **69** **Ta** Tangerine Dream	**62** **72** **Sy** Styx
51 **69** **Vg** Van der Graaf Generator	**57** **69** **Kc** King Crimson	**63** **82** **A** Asia

UFO

UFO's bridging position in this Periodic Table bears witness to their own heavy-rock trajectory: they started out as heads, and quickly became head-bangers.

Would-be astral voyagers who formed in London in 1969, their name was a homage to the capital's legendary hippy club that regularly held gigs, sorry, *happenings* by space cadets such as Pink Floyd and Soft Machine. Yet when UFO's own psychedelic career failed to get off the launch pad, the band rapidly took a pragmatic right-turn into more conventional heavy metal, recruiting 19-year-old former Scorpions guitarist Michael Schenker and allowing him to lavish his nimble-fingered, heavy-duty guitar-hero shtick all over albums with titles like *Force It* and *No Heavy Petting*.

Betraying their roots, UFO were by now one of hard rock's more primitive and less complex compounds and so America began to take a passing interest, but when star player Schenker split and headed *zurück* to the Scorpions in 1979, their album sales dipped. Heads down and thrashing away, UFO simply ploughed on, a long way from the most incandescent firework in rock's firmament but able to tour at a decent level and a regular fixture halfway down the bill at heavy-metal festivals.

The mercurial but erratic Schenker re-joined the band twice only to quit again both times, Jason Bonham passed through their ranks, and their journeyman rock was by now very much of the does-what-it-says-on-the-tin variety: professional, efficient, and about as cosmic as a tin of baked beans.

YES

Heavy rock ain't heavy rock if it doesn't possess at least one, ideally more, of three prime qualities: volume, velocity and virtuosity. Yes, the quintessential English progressive hard rockers, can do all three, but have always been primarily about the closing element.

Formed in London in 1968 by singer Jon Anderson and bassist Chris Squire, they were initially partly defined by the propulsive acid/freak rock of Pink Floyd and Cream, but soon spiralled off into a different galaxy. Prog's mantra was breaking down boundaries, and Yes's audaciously expansive eclecticism pulled folk, jazz and even classical music tropes into the mix, while never neglecting volume or velocity.

Their self-named 1969 debut album found them essaying psychedelic freak-out reshapings of the Byrds and the Beatles, but by 1971's *The Yes Album* they were playing all original material with such vast, exhaustive, cluttered instrumentation that you expected the instrument credits to include a kitchen sink.

Yet even this material appeared quaintly minimalist when Rick Wakeman joined the band, lugging with him his massed banks of organs, pianos, synthesisers and mellotron. Wakeman toughed up Yes's sound on albums such as the colossal *Fragile*, yet was then marginalised as Anderson wrenched the mysticism, sci-fi and quantum gibberish factor up to 11.

The apotheosis of this approach was 1973's 80-minute, four-tracks-long double album *Tales From Topographic Oceans*, a dense, hyper-elaborate travelogue across blasted distant sonic planets that delighted their global audience of stoned students more than it did Wakeman, who reacted by quitting the band (returning three years later).

Yes have noodled on ever since, not only a notable alloy in our Periodic Table, but arguably the band who over the years have attracted more chemistry-student fans than any other group extant.

EMERSON, LAKE & PALMER

Research chemists have always sought to broaden the sweep of human knowledge by means of laboratory experiments. In the 1970s, certain hubris-driven heavy rockers, some of whom apparently fancied themselves to be on a similar intellectual plane, did likewise.

Like bluesy tectonic plates shifting to form a fresh continent, Emerson, Lake & Palmer formed when the keyboardist of the Nice, Keith Emerson, recruited King Crimson singer/guitarist Greg Lake and powerhouse tyro drummer of Atomic Rooster, Carl Palmer, to form what *Melody Maker* in those days loved to call a 'supergroup'.

The trio played their second gig in front of 500,000 people at the Isle of Wight festival 1970, supporting Jimi Hendrix. Keith Emerson harboured the barely disguised ambition to be heavy rock's Hendrix of the keyboards, indulging in cosmic synthesiser solos on ELP's albums, while live only logistical restrictions and the danger of electrical conflagration stopped him from showily playing his instruments with his teeth before setting fire to them.

The band majored in portentous, pseudo-baroque episodic electro-symphonies, rock that was heavy in every respect except for rowdy guitar workouts. Even that deficiency was rectified on ELP's high-watermark 1973 magnum opus, *Brain Salad Surgery*, an album that introduced quasi-metal riffing to their fantastical space rock and featured abstruse adaptations of both 'Jerusalem' and Argentine composer Alberto Ginastera's 1st piano concerto.

It was little wonder that Emerson, Lake & Palmer came to be seen in some quarters as the epitome of self-important, ego-driven, masturbatory pomp rock, with the late DJ John Peel drily dismissing them as 'a waste of time, talent and electricity'. Sharing Peel's mindset, punk rockers viewed ELP as an archaic laughing stock and the group gave up and split in 1979, waiting until the safety of the 1990s to re-form.

GENESIS

From the elaborate stage sets and costumes of the first wave of progressive rockers to the pyrotechnics and upside-down crosses favoured by metallers to Spinal Tap's malfunctioning pods, heavy rock frequently cleaves towards the theatrical – and few have been more thespian than Genesis.

Formed in the mid-1960s in the rarefied climes of Charterhouse public school, as adolescents they embraced a strain of whimsical, folk-tinged prog rock that nodded towards Syd Barrett-era Pink Floyd, yet from 1971's *Nursery Cryme* album on their signature element was increasingly the arch, melodramatic singing style and theatrical live styling of front man Peter Gabriel.

Fond of death-white make-up, pagan costumes and delivering pedagogic onstage lectures contextualising the band's songs, Gabriel's am-dram indulgences peaked on *The Lamb Lies Down On Broadway*, Genesis's 1974 double-album rock opera/concept piece about (as far as you could tell) a Puerto Rican immigrant swept into a diabolic underground in New York. Gabriel had penned the entirety of the complex, cryptic narrative, which caused tensions within the band, and after a tour where Gabriel's characters included the Slipperman, a big-balled naked monster, the singer quit.

Phil Collins came out from behind the drums to take over as a rather folksier front man, and after a transitional period where Genesis reverted to their folky, prog-rock roots, they then largely eschewed such leanings and became a full-on slick pop-rock group, rubbing shoulders with Journey and Foreigner in the arenas of America and enjoying saccharine, sugar-rush MTV-friendly hits like 'Follow You, Follow Me' and 'Invisible Touch'.

Yet on a scientific level, it was hard not to conclude that when Peter Gabriel left, removing the eccentricity and pretension from Genesis, he also took the soul.

TANGERINE DREAM

Some purists may shudder at the contentious presence of Tangerine Dream on this Periodic Table of heavy rock: dude, where are the guitars? They hardly, like, rock at all! But these German electro-pioneers merit inclusion firstly for their beginnings as a far-flung, Teutonic wing of the progressive acid rock emanating from London and California in the late 1960s, and mostly because their music was heavy in the most elemental and vital sense: profound, questing, and ripe with meaning and layers of implication.

Their primary lines of musical attack and investigation may have been Moog synthesisers and sequencers rather than flying-V Gibson guitars and drums solos but they shared the expansive, curious, questing ethos that also powered Jimi Hendrix, Cream and Led Zeppelin: like Pink Floyd, their controls were set at warp speed for the heart of the sun.

Yet if Tangerine Dream appeared initially to flirt with space rock and the outré reaches of the counter-culture, despite their transparent disinterest in and even distaste for rock and roll, they soon headed off into their own musical orbit, writing screes of increasingly rich and rarefied trance-like instrumental symphonies, such as the *Phaedra* album, that won them chart success and a huge cult following.

Tangerine Dream might have forged a singular and most non-hard-rock route out of the sixties' dream but their avowed purity, idealism and sense of experimentation was truer to it than virtually any of their peers. Until his death in January 2015 aged 70, band founder and chief dreamer Edgar Froese pursued his own singular philosophical and electro-psychedelic vision – and many heavy-rock bands took notice.

KING CRIMSON

It's debatable whether King Crimson belong in a heavy-rock Periodic Table or are better viewed as an arcane branch of quantum physics. Quintessential cerebral prog rockers, they were not prone to wild guitar workouts or pile-driving percussion, yet it is impossible to view them as anything other than viscerally, all-pervasively heavy.

Founded by and around alchemical guitarist Robert Fripp, the group has seen something like 20 members pass through its ranks over its near 50-year, 25-album career, and yet its defining, indeed definitive, statement remains its debut. 1969's *In The Court Of The Crimson King* was a captivating mission statement, a neo-surrealist concept album (although it would be a brave soul who attempted to deconstruct or explain its narrative) that went a step further than any progressive rock contemporary in eschewing bluesy rhythms in favour of jazz and classical tropes.

The five pieces that made up its three-quarters-of-an hour duration were episodic, picaresque mini-symphonies, while Ian McDonald's thrumming mellotron suffused the music as tellingly as did Fripp's alternately apocalyptic and subtle guitar.

You could read multiple layers of meaning into *In The Court Of The Crimson King*, and joint-toking students across the globe did exactly that. Yet King Crimson were a most unstable and far from cohesive compound, with Fripp seemingly unable to hold down the same line-up of the band for two albums running: Greg Lake sang on 1970's *In The Wake Of Poseidon* before quitting to join Emerson, Lake & Palmer.

As numerous musos entered and exited as the decades went by, King Crimson became increasingly about Robert Fripp's singular musical vision – but he is a mad scientist always worth listening to.

Waste
Gases

Moving across the chemical Periodic Table and nearing its right-hand extremity, the metals are supplanted by non-metals, halogens and gases. As in science, so in heavy rock.

In America in the late 1970s and the 1980s, a mutant strain of music emerged that saw hard rock and progressive rock acts increasingly sanding off their more abrasive edges in favour of a more commercial, radio-friendly sound.

It worked, and bands such as REO Speedwagon, Foreigner, Journey and Styx soon became regulars on the US's enormo-dome circuit. While still nominally heavy, and with guitar and drum solos utterly mandatory, such acts nevertheless appeared essentially lightweight: so much hot air.

Retaining the bombast of the hoariest of progressive rockers yet jettisoning the musical experimentation, this flatulent music felt so calibrated for arena consumption that it even became labelled as such: arena rock. It attracted further labels, all of them derogatory: Adult-Orientated Rock (AOR), pomp rock, corporate rock.

It is fair to say this was not heavy rock's finest moment – and it was to cause a fissure in our Periodic Table...

Column 14

52 70 **U** UFO	58 75 **J** Journey	64 73 **Ae** Aerosmith
53 69 **Ys** Yes	59 77 **Fr** Foreigner	65 74 **K** Kiss
54 70 **E** Emerson, Lake & Palmer	60 71 **Ro** REO Speedwagon	66 69 **Ac** Alice Cooper
55 69 **G** Genesis	61 76 **Bt** Boston	67 67 **Db** David Bowie
56 69 **Ta** Tangerine Dream	62 72 **Sy** Styx	68 69 **Mt** Mott the Hoople
57 69 **Kc** King Crimson	63 82 **A** Asia	69 77 **Ml** Meat Loaf

JOURNEY

Forming in San Francisco in 1973, Journey began by majoring in a strain of jazz-rock fusion that betrayed the fact that two of their members were previously in Santana. The results were commercially underwhelming, and in 1977 they recruited a new singer, Steve Perry, and struck out in a far rockier and heavier direction.

Their breakthrough album was 1981's *Escape*, which topped the US chart, went on to sell 12 million copies and spawned hits like the anthemic power ballad 'Don't Stop Believin'' (rehabilitated by *Glee* 30 years later).

Hardcore followers of, say, Led Zeppelin or Black Sabbath inevitably regarded Journey as populist sell-outs recording vanilla Adult-Orientated Rock, but the band's album cuts had a far harder sheen and edge than their sops to the charts and their live gigs remained surprisingly intense, hard-riffing affairs.

If anything, they typified the phenomenon of the 1970s and 1980s whereby hard-rock-inclined bands grasped that injecting their tunes with overt pop hooks and melodies could catapult them from the club and theatre circuit they had slogged round for years into arenas.

Yet these aspirational bands had to be careful not to alienate their core rock audience: Journey's later 1980s albums saw them head towards a softer, sicklier and more sentimental keyboard-driven musical mush; they were notably less successful, and the band split in 1987.

FOREIGNER

In 1977, while Britain was reverberating to the Sex Pistols and Clash, America was getting down to the more streamlined sound of Foreigner and their debut single, 'Cold As Ice'.

Like many of the arena rock bands who were their musical and spiritual contemporaries, the New York-based Foreigner twigged there was money to be made in heavy rock with its more agitated edges discreetly jettisoned. The group's British founder and guitarist Mick Jones had previously been a jobbing musician, playing with George Harrison, Peter Frampton and Spooky Tooth, and this pragmatic approach showed when his first line-up of Foreigner featured former members of both Ian Hunter's band and King Crimson.

The success of 'Cold As Ice' ensured that Foreigner hit the ground running and in no time they were up and away, releasing album after album of carefully judged semi-hard rock and taking it to the world's arenas. Yet you can neither please nor, indeed, fool all of the people all of the time, and Foreigner's propensity for hitting big with windy, saccharine power ballads such as 'Waiting For A Girl Like You' and 'I Want To Know What Love Is' led to some of their earthier fans falling out of love with them. They were frustrated that while Jones produced albums by Bad Company and Van Halen in his spare time from the band, he showed zero interest in importing their raucous attitude into Foreigner's own measured take on heavy rock.

REO SPEEDWAGON

Anybody stumbling across REO Speedwagon's eponymous 1971 debut album would have figured them as just another anonymous group of American hard rockers. Rudimentary but rugged guitarist Gary Richrath ladled bluesy boogie riffs by the yard over raunchy numbers like 'Lay Me Down' and 'Prison Women' while '157 Riverside Avenue' was a lewd high-five celebrating an on-the-road conquest. So far, so ho hum, but it wasn't gonna buy no mansions.

The Illinois band went through various line-up changes through the 1970s as they searched for a winning chemical formula, but hit gold dust when they recruited folk-inclined singer Kevin Cronin. Cronin was a driving force as they dialled down the head-banging blues and dialled up the FM radio-friendly melodies and shoulder-heaving power ballads.

REO Speedwagon still rocked, and the excruciatingly named 1978 album *You Can Tune A Piano But You Can't Tuna Fish* remained loud and lairy, but everything changed on 1980's *Hi Infidelity*. Targeted firmly at the world's arenas, it hit its targets with forensic efficiency, going on to sell close on 10 million copies and spawning two inescapable power-ballad earworms in 'Keep On Loving You' and 'Take It On The Run'.

Were REO Speedwagon still heavy rock? Sort of, but their demographic shifted from denim-shirted longhairs to couples who only did two gigs per year, and with this came a corresponding image shift where they were viewed as irredeemably unhip. They merely sighed, carried on counting their money, and were last seen happily milking the millennial nostalgia circuit with their fellow arena-rock staples Styx, Journey and Foreigner.

BOSTON

61   76
Bt
Boston

The cover art alone of Boston's self-named 1976 debut album confirms that they were spiritually in hock to progressive rockers such as Yes, Emerson, Lake & Palmer and Genesis, and the group's main founder, songwriter, guitarist and guru, Tom Scholz, was as meticulous and perfectionist an operator as any of them.

Yet his prodigious talents were exercised in a far more populist direction. If a major theme of the time was canny bands appropriating heavy rock's adrenalin rush but replacing its abrasiveness with anthemic melodies and radio-friendly choruses, Boston were firmly in the vanguard.

The very first track on that debut album was that deadly but deliberate classic rock-guitar workout 'More Than A Feeling' and there were plenty more where that came from, as the studious Scholz designed his own studio equipment in order to capture the mellifluous melodies in his head.

The record quickly became the best-selling debut in US rock history and Boston's ecstatic record label, Epic, begged them for more product, but the fastidious Scholz kept them waiting for two years (a long time in those bang-'em-out days) as he micro-produced its follow-up, *Don't Look Back*, which also went to number 1. This delay was a mere rehearsal for what was to come as Scholz spent eight years on Boston's next magnum opus. Epic lost patience and sued them for breach of contract for taking so long to make it.

In the subsequent 29 years, Scholz and Boston have managed to record the grand total of three – yes, three – albums, to vastly diminishing returns.

STYX

The weighty progressive rock formulated by the likes of Yes and Emerson, Lake & Palmer had its merits but troubling the singles-chart compilers was not among them. Chicago rockers Styx began in the early 1970s heavily indebted to those bands' epic symphonies but had to take a more direct route to find sales success.

Recruiting singer Tommy Shaw in 1975, they embarked on a far more heavy-duty classic-rock direction as they looked to seduce the FM-radio producers of this world. Given the tenor of the times, they found the easiest way to do this was via power ballads.

However, after one particularly lachrymose and sentiment-sodden example of the genre, 'Babe', became their biggest hit to date, some members of the band mutinied and claimed they were betraying their hard-rock instincts. As the arguments raged, the guilty party who had written 'Babe', co-vocalist and keyboardist Dennis DeYoung, even quit the group for a while.

When tempers cooled and they were all back in the room, Styx reverted to their earlier theatrical prog rock leanings with a concept album, *Paradise Theater*, that looked to take the temperature of Reagan-era America. Its follow-up, *Kilroy Was Here*, even embraced that last resort of the scoundrel progressive rocker, science fiction, borrowing heavily from Rush's *2112*.

With their heavy-rock tendencies firmly sidelined, sales declining and members squabbling, Styx disappeared up their own fundaments and split in 1984.

ASIA

63		82
	A	
	Asia	

Were heavy rock measured by weight of reputation, Asia would have tipped the scales at the proverbial 16 tons.

The British group coalesced in the early 1980s, a portentous merger of big-name refugees from the previous decade's progressive rock dinosaurs: Steve Howe and Geoff Downes (Yes), Carl Palmer (Emerson, Lake & Palmer) and John Wetton (King Crimson).

Their music was exactly what you would have expected a supergroup (as it seemed almost legally mandatory to refer to them) like this to sound like: heavy, yes, yet also bombastic, overladen, pompous and buffed to such a preposterous degree that you could see your horror-stricken face in it.

To Britain's credit it never really succumbed to Asia, but America was big on such slick, faux-meaningful dross at the time and the band's self-titled 1982 debut album annexed the top of the Billboard chart for two months and was the biggest-selling record of that year.

Given this phenomenal, and some might say inexplicable, success, Asia naturally attempted to repeat the exact formula with the following year's *Alpha*, but it all went a tad wrong in the laboratory this time around. The pomp-rock synths, flatulent bluster and gale-force gibberish lyrics far outweighed any heavy-rock content, and although *Alpha* was again a platinum seller, their singer John Wetton was so disenchanted that he quit the band.

The rock world had by now moved on but poor, befuddled Asia failed to notice, and for the next 15 years they released a string of similarly titled pomp-rock epics – *Astra, Aqua, Aria, Arena* and *Aura* – that virtually all failed even to squeeze into the US top 200.

Precious Gases
(some flammable)

This heavy-rock Periodic Table is not composed merely of gentle, gradual musical gradations and progression. Indeed, at this point it undergoes something of a schism, a rupture.

The majority of the elements in this chapter formed mainly (but not exclusively) in the second half of the 1970s, as a direct reaction to what preceded them. Appalled by the musical methane farted out by the bombastic progressive and arena rockers, heavy rock went in search of kicks.

Aerosmith and Meat Loaf were not without portentous moments but leavened them with bluesy menace and a keen, self-mocking sense of humour respectively. Kiss began their face-painted bid for world domination determined that each second they spent on stage should be more exciting than the one before it.

In Britain, Queen riffed hard and explored the outer fringes of high camp while David Bowie triggered the alien, cleverly outrageous glam-rock explosion. The Sex Pistols declared war on rock's old order; a whole wave of angry, attitudinal punk-metal bands followed in their wake.

They were heavy, but unlike the lumbering dinosaurs they made extinct, these musical precious gases were also nimble, sharp, dexterous, as light as air. Hard rock had received an injection of wit and humour. It had certainly needed it.

Column 15

58 **75** **J** Journey	**64** **73** **Ae** Aerosmith	**70** **73** **Qu** Queen
59 **77** **Fr** Foreigner	**65** **74** **K** Kiss	**71** **73** **Ny** New York Dolls
60 **71** **Ro** REO Speedwagon	**66** **69** **Ac** Alice Cooper	**72** **82** **Ts** Twisted Sister
61 **76** **Bt** Boston	**67** **67** **Db** David Bowie	**73** **71** **Sw** Sweet
62 **72** **Sy** Styx	**68** **69** **Mt** Mott the Hoople	**74** **69** **Sl** Slade
63 **82** **A** Asia	**69** **77** **Ml** Meat Loaf	**75** **73** **Qa** Suzi Quatro

64	73
Ae	
Aerosmith	

AEROSMITH

One of America's biggest and most totemic bands, Aerosmith have always cannily known exactly when to leaven their bluesy, metallic riffing with a soaring melody or an arena-pleasing chorus.

Their slick forte has always been a strain of rootsy, hard-edged anthemic rock with pop smarts, a formula not a million miles from the Rolling Stones, and, indeed, singer Steven Tyler's pouting, elbow-flapping simian strut has always made for a stunningly accurate Mick Jagger impersonation.

Originally a heads-down power trio of Tyler, guitarist Joe Perry and drummer Tom Hamilton, Aerosmith formed in 1970, grew to a five-piece and paid their dues on the circuit, supporting both Mott the Hoople and the Kinks before scoring their major breakthrough with their third album, 1975's *Toys In The Attic*.

It was a magnificently trashy and raunchy record that combined Tyler and Perry's potent predilection for lewd sexual innuendo with some heavy-duty riffing that, to say the least, owed a major stylistic debt to Led Zeppelin.

The difference? Whereas the Stones and Zep had political and/or spiritual dimensions, Aerosmith were very much here to party, as tracks like 'Walk This Way' and 'Sweet Emotion' made clear.

Indeed, Tyler and Perry partied rather too hard over the next decade, going into a hedonistic spiral that culminated in the pair slumping into rehab in the mid-1980s. Yet, nothing if not survivors, Aerosmith never stopped being popular, and on their newly sober return they enjoyed a remarkable second wind, partly due to their sharp mastery of that most maligned, melodramatic let's-slow-it-down hard-rock medium, the power ballad.

Diamond has long been held to be the hardest element known to science. Aerosmith are equally indestructible.

KISS

Without being American, it's impossible fully to appreciate the importance and influence of Kiss on US rock history and pop culture. Musically competent but scarcely innovative, they nevertheless became game-changing, commercial colossi by dint of brilliant image management and a razor-sharp eye for business and marketing opportunities.

The band's musical influences were blatant from the off: the pantomime horror show of Alice Cooper and the attitudinal, punky sneer of the New York Dolls. Yet while lacking the originality of either of these touchstones, they effortlessly surpassed their album sales and magazine column inches by commoditising themselves to within an inch of their lives.

Kiss's music was efficient, sporadically rousing hard rock with sing-a-long choruses bespoke for arenas, but America's wide-eyed teens were equally wooed by its slick packaging. Festooned in preposterous, vivid costumes and industrial layers of face paint, they were a cartoon conceptualised by their Svengali-like bassist and leader, Gene Simmons.

As their status grew during the 1970s, their Kiss Army fan club peaked at 100,000 members, and the opportunistic Simmons never missed a trick when it came to flogging them increasingly far-fetched and unlikely merchandise: Kiss dolls, robots, knives, condoms and in 2001, ironically noting the ageing demographic of their fan base, the Kiss funeral casket (sorry, kasket).

Yet scratch away the face paint and they are one of this table's more basic elements: iconic and legendary they may be, yet it's still hard not to regard Kiss as a gimlet-eyed marketing strategy with a smart band attached.

ALICE COOPER

Heavy rock has always had its shock-terrorists and taboo-testers but it was Alice Cooper who forcibly wrenched open Pandora's (dressing-up) box.

Armed with a story about the band's name having been gifted to him during a Ouija board session (which he later admitted was rubbish) and inspired by Bette Davis's trowel-it-all-over approach to facial make-up in *What Ever Happened To Baby Jane*, the Detroit native born Vincent Furnier launched his band in the late 1960s, as inspired by horror movies as he was by the bluesy riffs of the Doors and the Rolling Stones.

From the outset, Alice Cooper's shtick and USP were his theatricality and vaudeville noir; at his grotesque-carnival live shows, Cooper was strapped into an electric chair and baby dolls were regularly decapitated on guillotines in showers of fake blood as (real) boa constrictors roamed around the stage and on Cooper's shoulders.

His music began as an interesting amalgam of blues, pop-rock and even Beatles-like psychedelia before morphing into more basic, utilitarian heavy metal in the early 1970s as his founding band split and he continued, while giving himself the band's name.

Furnier was a preacher's son and this may possibly have occasioned psychological issues that he carried into his wanton, establishment-baiting music; the 'School's Out' single thrilled education-hating adolescents everywhere, while his commercial high-water mark, 1973's *Billion Dollar Babies*, hit number 1 on both sides of the Atlantic and spawned 'No More Mr. Nice Guy', 'Elected' and the distinctly unpleasant 'Raped And Freezin''.

While never quite equalling the success of this tabloid-shocking imperial period, Cooper has remained the arena-filling godfather of panto-metal, helping to spawn Kiss, Mötley Crüe, Marilyn Manson and many, many more.

DAVID BOWIE

It feels counter-intuitive to think of David Bowie as a heavy rocker. Sure, he has flirted with the genre over the years, as he has with hippy-folk, space-rock, glam, stadium-filling art-pop, blue-eyed soul and techno, but surely the ultimate musical chameleon is far too elusive to be tethered to this Periodic Table?

And yet Bowie merits inclusion because of the legions of overawed rockers and metal freaks who have taken inspiration from him. Even only dabbling in heavy rock, he became a shaping element. After that awkward teenage whimsical folk-and-mime period that we all go through, he reinvented himself as a bluesy rocker on 1970's largely unsuccessful *The Man Who Sold The World* album, and returned to the format in the late 1980s both solo and with the critically slated Tin Machine project.

Nobody sane, though, would describe these as David Bowie's finest moments. His imperial period came in the early 1970s, when he released a slew of febrile, fantastical glam-rock albums in *Hunky Dory, The Rise and Fall of Ziggy Stardust and the Spiders from Mars* and *Aladdin Sane* that, beneath the jaw-dropping futuristic narratives and fantastical musical invention, also rocked like demons – the elbow grease of dogged guitarist Mick Ronson made sure of that.

Were Bowie's musical fictions mere lightweight fancies with no propulsive heft, no graft and gravitas, they would never have inspired countless armies of glam and heavy rockers from Freddie Mercury to Gene Simmons to Perry Farrell to Marilyn Manson as profoundly as they did.

Pop music is David Bowie's world, and every one else is allowed to play in it: heavy rock is as indebted to him as is any other genre, and arguably more than most.

MOTT THE HOOPLE

The perennial nearly men, Mott the Hoople are among the heavy-rock artists whose legend and influence far outweigh their commercial success.

In truth, they always were a cult property, attracting critical hosannas and a fervent word-of-mouth live following with their early releases which merged ferocious yet angular hard-rock riffing with the scabrous, almost Dylan-like oblique lyrical observations of singer Ian Hunter.

A 1971 gig at the Royal Albert Hall led to a riot that caused the venerable venue to ban rock shows for years, yet Mott's rave reviews simply didn't translate to record sales, and the band were famously on the verge of splitting when David Bowie lent a hand.

A major fan of Mott's gnomic blues, Bowie gave them a killer track in 'All The Young Dudes', produced their 1972 album of the same name and, tellingly, persuaded them to don glam clobber. Bowie's help inspired the band to hone their own songwriting chops, and the album hit big on both sides of the Atlantic.

Finally, Mott the Hoople were actually rock stars, and characteristically they celebrated the fact by releasing a meta concept album, *Mott*, about the piquancy and bathos of being in a band. *Mott* spawned the delicious, classic glam-rock single 'All The Way From Memphis' and its follow-up, *The Hoople*, produced 'Roll Away The Stone' but by now the band were squabbling, and founder member and guitarist Mick Ralphs quit in a huff to form the far earthier Bad Company.

Numerous line-up changes followed, but when the quixotic, talismanic Hunter quit to form a duo with Bowie guitarist Mick Ronson, the end was in sight. A potent compound, Mott burned with intensity... but ultimately they burned out.

MEAT LOAF

Meat Loaf is where the conceptualisations of progressive rock meet the cheesiness of musical theatre.

Through the 1970s, larger-than-life Texan Marvin Lee Aday birthed a series of preposterous, bombastic and hugely enjoyable mini-rock operas with his songwriter partner-in-crime Jim Steinman. Aday had pretty much fallen into his Meat Loaf persona: his early career was a ragbag CV including acting stints in the musical *Hair* and the cult movie *The Rocky Horror Picture Show*, and an unfortunate spell singing vocals for Ted Nugent.

Yet when he reunited with occasional cohort Steinman for 1977's *Bat Out Of Hell* album, everything fell into place. Produced by Todd Rundgren, the record was a concept piece, but whereas Yes were trying to sketch *Tales From Topographic Oceans*, Meat Loaf and Steinman's narrative appeared to unfold in an adolescent world of gothic graphic comics.

Epic, audacious and corny as, well, hell, hyperventilating tracks such as 'You Took The Words Right Out Of My Mouth', 'Two Out Of Three Ain't Bad' and 'Paradise By The Dashboard Light' could have rung from the soundtrack of *Rocky Horror* and nobody would have batted a mascaraed eyelid. If you were to squint a little, you could hear traces of the Who's *Tommy*, the Doors's cod poetry and even Bruce Springsteen in there, but really Meat Loaf existed in his own musical universe.

Bat Out Of Hell has sold more than 40 million copies worldwide, and the only time Meat Loaf and Steinman came remotely close to reproducing its success was when they returned to the formula for 1993's *Bat Out Of Hell II: Back Into Hell*. If a chemical formula's not broken, don't fix it.

Column 16

64 73 ## Ae Aerosmith	**70 73** ## Qu Queen	**76 87** ## Gu Guns N' Roses
65 74 ## K Kiss	**71 73** ## Ny New York Dolls	**77 94** ## Mm Marilyn Manson
66 69 ## Ac Alice Cooper	**72 82** ## Ts Twisted Sister	**78 77** ## Sx Sex Pistols
67 67 ## Db David Bowie	**73 71** ## Sw Sweet	**79 77** ## Dm Damned
68 69 ## Mt Mott the Hoople	**74 69** ## Sl Slade	**80 84** ## Cu Cult
69 77 ## Ml Meat Loaf	**75 73** ## Qa Suzi Quatro	**81 03** ## Ds The Darkness

70	73
Qu	
Queen	

QUEEN

Queen were certainly heavy. The band's genesis lay in guitarist Brian May and drummer Roger Taylor's late 1960s hard-rock group Smile, and May was perennially capable of dispensing girder-like riffs with a casual flick of his wrist.

Nevertheless, in certain purist rock circles, Queen never received the kudos afforded to lesser lights such as Deep Purple or Bad Company. What were their crimes? They dared to flaunt a pop sensibility, enjoy a string of pop hits and be, well, fun.

Queen could, and did, rock out with the best of them – just consider their live favourite 'Tie Your Mother Down', driven by May's pulverising Black Sabbath-like riff – but their take on heavy rock was more baroque, subversive and bombastic, embodied in their flamboyant and high-camp front man Freddie Mercury.

They may have started off in hock to the blues, like so many bands of their era, but by 1975's *A Night At The Opera* they had excised virtually every vestige of hoary old R&B from their sound in favour of the flippant dynamics and wham-bam-thank-you-ma'am! rambunctiousness of glam rock.

Queen were macho enough to appeal to the denim-clad 1970s troglodyte hordes – their badge nestled on many a Levi's and Wrangler jacket, next to that of Status Quo – but the just-about-in-the-closet Mercury's persona owed as much to Liza Minnelli as it did to Ozzy Osbourne.

The epic episodic, faux-operatic single 'Bohemian Rhapsody', complete with its 180 vocal overdubs, was as audacious and preposterous as 'Stairway To Heaven', yet unlike Led Zeppelin, Queen's tongue was planted firmly in their cheek.

May's muscular guitar and the group's robust, rigorous musicality earned them the often-grudging respect of the head-banging hordes, but at heart Queen were a gang of bicep-flexing pop tarts.

NEW YORK DOLLS

Brian Eno famously said of the Velvet Underground that hardly anybody bought their records, but virtually every one who did so went on to form a band. If there is a similar entity in the hard-rock/heavy-metal pantheon, it is the New York Dolls.

Just as hypnotised as Aerosmith's Steven Tyler by Mick Jagger's apeman strut and dandyish chic, stardust vocalist David Johansen and guitarist Johnny Thunders formed the Dolls in New York in 1971 in an androgynous riot of lipstick, ripped stockings, stack heels and trashy riffs that gained them a devoted – but small – cult following, and had major record companies running for the hills. Their infamy grew further when drummer Billy Murcia overdosed and died on a tour of England.

Their eponymous 1973 album, with its monochrome cover of the band in drag and ragged, glorious outbursts of song such as 'Personality Crisis', was well received by critics despite its spectacularly rudimentary musicianship but this enthusiasm was not shared by the record-buying public. The same fate befell its follow-up, the gleefully anarchic *Too Much Too Soon*, at which point the band's label unceremoniously dumped them.

The original one-chord, attitude-heavy wonders, the Dolls are often called the first punk rock band, and their sometime manager Malcolm McLaren certainly took visual and attitudinal cues from his charges when he returned to London and turned his attention to the Sex Pistols (the Ramones were listening pretty hard, too).

The New York Dolls's mythology grew as they split up, succumbed to drug habits (Thunders died of an OD in 1991) then miraculously re-formed after long-time fan Morrissey invited them to play his Meltdown Festival in London in 2004. Prophets without honour for far too long, their recognition came very late – but at least it came.

72	82
Ts	
Twisted Sister	

TWISTED SISTER

Twisted Sister are a chemical-enabling element, a gateway-drug band that bridged the divide between New York art-punk and the heavier, more Spandex-laden hair metal that later infested the West Coast.

Springing up out of Long Island in the early 1970s, Twisted Sister were initially utterly in thrall to the camp, glam posturing of the New York Dolls, shadowing their every move so faithfully that they were in danger of being a tribute band.

They only left this wide-eyed idolatry behind when their ranks were swelled by a charismatic new vocalist, Dee Snider, with a determined vision of the group as a far more hard-edged, metallic affair. Early singles such as 'I'll Never Grow Up, Now!' and 'Bad Boys (Of Rock 'n' Roll)' didn't so much flirt with self-parody as roger it senseless, but Twisted Sister's early 1980s albums *You Can't Stop Rock 'n' Roll* and *Stay Hungry* crossed over from their punk-metal cult following to mainstream success due to MTV playing the knockabout, slapstick videos to 'We're Not Gonna Take It' and 'I Wanna Rock' to death.

Yet some hard-rock compounds are less stable than others, and Twisted Sister soon suffered an identity crisis – were they the edgy art-rockers who had idolised New York Dolls, or painted, costumed clowns to cheer the masses à la Kiss?

Confused albums that attempted to please both elements of their audience failed to satisfy either, and lambasted as hapless sell-outs by hardcore fans and critics alike, Twisted Sister gave up and split before the decade was over – although an unexpected, re-formed version of the band is nowadays being indulged by heavy-metal festival crowds.

73	71
Sw	
Sweet	

SWEET

The Sweet were initially unremarkable British heavy rockers who then opportunistically forged a career as part of the early 1970s glam-rock scene dreamed up by

David Bowie and Marc Bolan. They even came complete with their own Svengalis: the songwriting duo of Nicky Chinn and Mike Chapman, who saw which way the wind was blowing and poured their charges into pink satin trousers and sequinned jackets. It worked like a dream and the Sweet enjoyed a string of irresistible early 1970s chart hits that married bubblegum-pop hooks, crunching hard-rock riffs and innuendo-laden lyrical content that implied that Chinn and Chapman were either taking inspiration from saucy seaside postcards, or employing Benny Hill as a consultant (check out the lyric sheet for 'Little Willy' or 'Wig-Wam Bam').

Yet while they always looked like brickies in drag on *Top of the Pops*, the Sweet's true roots lay in heavy rock – their live shows and self-penned material were far weightier than their chart hits, and the mid-1970s saw them mutiny against their all-powerful mentors and insist on writing their own singles.

It was a shame: the Sweet were fantastic fun when their driving riffs were alleviated by Chinn and Chapman's surging choruses and pop magic, and when they reverted to head-banging type, the record-buying public rapidly lost interest.

As soon as punk rock changed the UK's musical landscape, the Sweet faded from the radar and came to a fairly ignominious end, but a decade later the insidious effect of their lewd rock could be detected in US glam-metallers such as Mötley Crüe, Ratt and Poison.

SLADE

David Bowie isn't just an integral element in rock's Periodic Table but one capable of altering the very composition and structure of the matter next to him.

Slade were little more than a Wolverhampton pub band with a handful of failed releases behind them in 1971 when they decided to clump aboard the Bowie-led glam-rock bandwagon. They adopted his cosmic, stardust ethos in a decidedly singular fashion, eschewing his sexual ambiguity in favour of visiting *Top of the Pops* in increasingly outlandish outfits that suggested not so much androgynous aliens as piss-taking lads raiding the dressing-up box.

From singer Noddy Holder's mirror-laden top hat to guitarist Dave Hill's metal nun's wimple, Slade were out to prompt not awe but belly laughs. Beneath the costumed japery, their music remained largely unaltered: a bluesy chug powered by lairy and lascivious riffs and titanic drumming, topped by the gruff bellow of asbestos-larynxed, Victorian sideburn-toting Holder, whose vocal suggested a man trying to attract the attention of somebody two streets away.

Slade looked like boorish yobs who were in the right place at the right time and couldn't believe their luck, playing up to that image with a series of deliberately misspelt song titles: 'Coz I Luv You', 'Take Me Bak 'Ome', 'Mama Weer All Crazee Now', 'Skweeze Me, Pleeze Me'. Yet this was misleading: a shrewd musical intelligence underlay their canny pop-metal hits, powered to the top of the charts by indelible hooks and rampaging choruses.

Certain chemical elements just don't travel, and America never 'got' Slade ('"Look Wot You Dun"? Huh?'), but in Britain their chart-strafing cartoon metal capers made them bona fide national treasures. Especially at Christmas.

SUZI QUATRO

Glam rock made stars of some of the most unlikely heavy rockers and Suzi Quatro was a beneficiary.

The 21-year-old Detroit native was singing with a bluesy band called Cradle on her local bar circuit in 1971 when visiting British music mogul and record producer Mickie Most happened across one of her gigs. Most signed her to his own RAK Records label, relocated her to London and fixed her up with songwriters Chapman and Chinn, who at the time were mostly engaged in churning out wham-bam-thank-you-glam! singles for the Sweet.

The two-man hit factory did the same for Quatro, who was soon riding high in the charts in Britain – but not in the US – with bubblegum-metal stompers like 'Can The Can', '48 Crash' and 'Devil Gate Drive'.

Yet Quatro was no mere malleable puppet: she was a full-on leather-jacketed Midwest rock chick and Most, Chinn and Chapman reflected that, ensuring that her hits appealed to head-bangers as well as pop kids. With Quatro, it was clear the platform boots and the Bolan pout were extras: she was all about the riffs and the volume.

Her fortunes were to get a boost in the States when she received the all-important support of the Fonz, making numerous cameo appearances in *Happy Days* as a somewhat typecast rock singer named Leather Tuscadero. After her star faded in the 1980s, Quatro turned to stage and TV acting and worked as a radio DJ but her musical achievements remain under-celebrated.

Just glance across our Periodic Table: heavy rock was always a man's game, and in the boorish, chauvinistic 1970s, the valiant Quatro ploughed a lonely and laudable furrow.

Column 17

			82 **Bj** 84 Bon Jovi
70 **Qu** 73 Queen	76 **Gu** 87 Guns N' Roses	83 **Mö** 81 Mötley Crüe	
71 **Ny** 73 New York Dolls	77 **Mm** 94 Marilyn Manson	84 **R** 84 Ratt	
72 **Ts** 82 Twisted Sister	78 **Sx** 77 Sex Pistols	85 **Pn** 86 Poison	
73 **Sw** 71 Sweet	79 **Dm** 77 Damned	86 **Wp** 84 W.A.S.P.	
74 **Sl** 69 Slade	80 **Cu** 84 Cult	87 **St** 84 Spinal Tap	
75 **Qa** 73 Suzi Quatro	81 **Ds** 03 Darkness	88 **Se** 09 Steel Panther	

GUNS N' ROSES

Who translated the classic bad-boy rock-and-roll swagger of the Rolling Stones and Aerosmith for the hair-metal generation? Easy: it was the walking chemical factory that was Guns N' Roses.

Emerging in the mid-1980s suffused in MTV's indulgent cathode glow, G N' R were precisely as rough-edged, leery and sleazy as you would hope from a band whose vocalist, Axl Rose, constructed his stage name as an anagram of oral sex.

Pitched at some profane point between Aerosmith's bluesy histrionics and the glam-metal of Mötley Crüe, whom they supported on a famously debauched 1987 tour, Guns translated a spoilt-brat, hugely entitled punk attitude into hard-edged, confrontational heavy rock. Top-hat-sporting, cigarette-chewing guitarist Slash was a mercurial alchemist, capable of unfurling riffs like febrile girders, while Rose was antsy, troubled white trash and defiant about it.

To the standard heavy-metal, moral-vacuum default positions of misogyny and sexism, Guns clumsily added racism and homophobia; the pig-ignorant 'One In A Million' barked 'Niggers and police, out of my way' and 'Immigrants and faggots, they make no sense to me' like a saloon-bar good ol' boy. Yet Rose was to repent that line, and Guns were never *evil*; just a tad dumb.

After 1987's *Appetite For Destruction* became the best-selling debut album of all time and its follow-ups *Use Your Illusion I* and *II* divided critics, it became apparent that Guns N' Roses lacked the chemical cohesion to survive their fame and notoriety and their members quit one by one, leaving angst-ridden, rogue particle Rose alone to spend 15 years brooding over the truly daft *Chinese Democracy* album.

It figured: this particular combustible compound was always going to end in tears.

MARILYN MANSON

In the early 1990s, a surprisingly high number of rock and metal's more antediluvian fans were still decrying any music that leaned heavily on electronics and synthesisers as 'pussy' and effeminate. Marilyn Manson put a stop to that.

The shy loner and social misfit born Brian Warner in smalltown Ohio set out making campy shock-horror music arguably as in debt to Jim Steinman and Meat Loaf as it was to Alice Cooper – his first album featured songs called 'Cake And Sodomy' and 'Dope Hat' – but his second offering, 1996's *Antichrist Superstar*, upped the ante severely. Its mix of Ministry-style industrial electronica, metal guitars and anti-establishment posturing brought him firmly into the rock world and into the remit of this Periodic Table, as well as earning him a big-break support tour with Nine Inch Nails.

Yet Manson's supreme talent was as an arch media manipulator and controversialist. Adopting 'Antichrist Superstar' as his alter ego and consequently finding his shows regularly picketed by evangelist Christian and right-wing pressure groups, he fanned the flames of their moral outrage magnificently via tracks such as 'I Don't Like The Drugs (But The Drugs Like Me)' and 'Irresponsible Hate Anthem'.

In the grand tradition of both Cooper and Ozzy Osbourne, Manson quickly became a hate figure for Middle America and loved it, although his affection for this role was doubtless somewhat neutered when he found his influence being absurdly blamed for the Columbine High School massacre of 1999.

Beneath the trowelled-on make-up and crunching electro-metal riffs, the suspicion remains that Marilyn Manson is an über-Goth pantomime villain – but he gives great headline.

SEX PISTOLS

Few of the original 1970s British punk bands could truly be described as heavy rockers. They appeared in a shudder of revulsion against the baroque and bombastic excesses of the progressive rockers that immediately preceded them: their short-sharp-shock, three-chord-wonder songs were the very obverse of Yes and Emerson, Lake & Palmer.

Yet punk's figureheads, the Sex Pistols, merit inclusion in this table both for the sheer heft of their vastly underrated guitarist Steve Jones's riffing, and for their seismic effect on the rock world that they were to revolutionise.

The Sex Pistols's own musical influences were negligible, if not spurious: 'We're not really into music, we're into chaos,' as Johnny Rotten was to sneer, while sporting an 'I Hate Pink Floyd' T-shirt: their nearest musical antecedents were the attitudinal overload and insurrection of fellow Brit malcontents the Who and the nihilistic noise of the Stooges, whom they occasionally covered.

Yet the Pistols's amateurish yet preternaturally spirited strain of garage rock sounded like pure aural adrenalin, the perfect platform for Rotten to issue his archly incendiary rallying calls against apathy and complacency. Provocation lay at the heart of their agenda, a trick that their manager, Malcolm McLaren, honed from his previous (unsuccessful) stint in charge of the New York Dolls.

The Sex Pistols were arguably the most unstable element of all the matter in this table, an antibody of chaos and confusion: the time span from Rotten's opening snarl of 'I am an anti-Christ, I am an anarchist!' on 'Anarchy In The UK' to his drawled 'Ever get the feeling that you've been cheated?' at their final gig in San Francisco's Winterland Ballroom was a mere 14 months.

Yet they didn't half make one hell of a Big Bang.

DAMNED

Underestimated in the UK due to their knockabout image, the Damned were where punk's skein-of-spittle adrenalin thrash met theatrical rock, and were a far heavier concern than is usually realised.

Bassist Ray Burns and drummer Chris Millar, who soon adopted the respective monikers Captain Sensible and Rat Scabies, were grubbing around in various London punk bands when they met vampiric singer Dave Vanian, an Alice Cooper and New York Dolls fan, whose devotion to the Goth ethos extended to having worked as a gravedigger (and whose own punk *nom de guerre* was a clumsy play on 'Transylvanian').

Ahead of the curve next to both the Sex Pistols and the Clash, the Damned have a strong claim to being safety-pinned pioneers, releasing both the first bona fide punk single in 1976's 'New Rose', and first album in the following year's *Damned Damned Damned*. Yet they were never *just* about punk – this first incarnation of the Damned packed enough glam punch and sense of mischief to also tour with T. Rex.

After a short split, they re-formed in 1978 with Captain Sensible now transferred to guitar and produced a series of witty, scabrous short-arm jabs to the solar plexus such as 'Love Song' and 'Smash It Up', while a cover of the Sweet's 'Ballroom Blitz' stressed their simultaneous love of mascara-toting, rocky bubblegum pop.

Live, they were hard, heavy and ferocious, as at home at metal festivals as they were at punk-rock shindigs: had it not been for Sensible's wacky antics and compulsive clowning, the Damned might have gone down in rock history as a British Alice Cooper, rather than as mere punk also-rans.

CULT

The Cult's precise location in this Periodic Table very much depends on which manifestation of the band we choose to focus on.

When singer Ian Astbury launched them as Southern Death Cult in Yorkshire in 1982, they were agitated, angst-ridden Goth rockers. The vocalist then split the band and formed Death Cult, before shortening the name further still to avoid being pigeonholed as Goths.

Yet once they had settled on the name the Cult, they found their line and length as more traditional hard rockers with traces of Led Zeppelin's gravitas and portentousness. They achieved the difficult task of crossing over from cult indie status to heavy-metal land while taking their original audience with them.

After scoring big in Britain in 1985 with the 'She Sells Sanctuary' single, two years later they made inroads into heavy rock's sacred land, America, with the *Electric* album. Their next album, 1989's *Sonic Temple*, was huge over there and it led to the Cult supporting Metallica and recruiting a future member of Guns N' Roses, Matt Sorum, into their ranks.

Yet throughout all of this success, Astbury carried a flame for his hero and role model: Jim Morrison. Similarly hung up on mysticism and fancying himself as a poetic shaman and emissary from the dark side, Astbury indulged his deep fascination with Native American spirituality and was prone to venting streams of freeform pseudo-portentous drivel at live shows.

When he split the Cult again in 2001 to join Morrison's former bandmates Robby Krieger and Ray Manzarek in the Doors of the 21st Century (aka Riders on the Storm), it was clearly Astbury's dream gig. The Primark Lizard King is now back with the Cult.

DARKNESS

Students of the science of rock know this: there is a thin line between tribute and parody, and it is occasionally difficult to know which side of the line – and, thus, whereabouts in this table – an artist lies.

Voilà – the Darkness! The band's legend claims singer Justin Hawkins discovered his vocation and calling while singing Queen's 'Bohemian Rhapsody' during a karaoke party, and certainly Freddie Mercury's histrionic, meta-camp singing style was a strong influence on Hawkins's own seemingly helium-fuelled falsetto.

Heavily in thrall to both 1970s glam poppers like the Sweet and 1980s melodic metallers such as Judas Priest, the Darkness rocked hard and loud, but their blatantly derivative shtick and innate flippancy led to them being seen as a joke by the UK's major record labels. This was fair enough; they were.

Yet they continued plugging away, and support tours with genuine old-school rock royalty Deep Purple and Def Leppard made hysterical (in all senses of the world) 2003 single 'Keep Your Hands Off My Woman' a minor British hit. A re-released signature song, 'I Believe In A Thing Called Love', was even a top 10 hit in America despite (or due to) sounding like Kiss on laughing gas, and when their debut album *Permission To Land* went to number 1 in the UK, the jokers looked to have had the last laugh.

Sadly, they were to mirror the career trajectory of so many of the flash-in-the-pan old-school rockers they mimicked: they released a stinker of a second album, *One Way Ticket To Hell... And Back*, that stiffed, and the hard-partying Hawkins then vanished into rehab for alcohol and cocaine addiction.

They have since returned – older, wiser, and rather less successful.

Ignoble Gases

The elements in the final column of the chemical Periodic Table were once known as the inert gases. That doesn't really work for our purposes. They were renamed the noble gases. That is even wider of the mark. Ignoble? Ah, now you're talking.

What's in a name? Is it hair metal? Glam metal? Either way, the fizzing, effervescent gases completing our main table are simultaneously heavy rock and lighter than air. They are metal's good time that is had by all, the poodle rockers who are arguably heavy rock's most polarising elements.

Critics have always disparaged Mötley Crüe, Poison and Ratt's chauvinism and misogyny and Bon Jovi's cartoon outlaw shtick, possibly missing the point that their tongues tend to be wedged firmly in their pouting cheeks. Mötley Crüe even invited Steel Panther, the forensically accurate spoof band whose preening bassist Lexxi Foxx bears more than a passing resemblance to Nikki Sixx, to support them.

And you don't do shit like that without a sense of humour.

Column 18

82 Bj 84
Bj
Bon Jovi

76 Gu 87	83 Mö 81
Gu	**Mö**
Guns N' Roses	Mötley Crüe

77 Mm 94	84 R 84
Mm	**R**
Marilyn Manson	Ratt

78 Sx 77	85 Pn 86
Sx	**Pn**
Sex Pistols	Poison

79 Dm 77	86 Wp 84
Dm	**Wp**
Damned	W.A.S.P.

80 Cu 84	87 St 84
Cu	**St**
Cult	Spinal Tap

81 Ds 03	88 Se 09
Ds	**Se**
Darkness	Steel Panther

BON JOVI

It is appropriate that Bon Jovi sit atop the lighter end of this table in the position normally occupied by helium, the tasteless gas inhaled at parties to generate funny voices.

In truth, many observers feel the band consist of little more than flatulent hot air. It was a harbinger to their future that founder and vocalist Jon Bon Jovi's first musical ventures consisted of recording radio jingles and singing 'R2-D2 We Wish You A Merry Christmas' on a *Star Wars* Christmas album.

Indeed, it is fair to say Mr Bon Jovi is not one of the purer elements in rock's chemical spectrum: his band took the name of their breakthrough 1986 album *Slippery When Wet* from a sign they saw on a visit to a Canadian strip club.

Although their propensity for widdly-widdly guitar solos and headlining Donington might appear to qualify Bon Jovi as heavy rockers, many might question whether this is true: they came to straddle 1980s rock like poodle-haired colossi by flogging a Disneyfied, family-friendly and MTV-dominating version of the infinitely more authentic strain of blue-collar romanticism peddled by their fellow New Jersey native, Bruce Springsteen.

It's no surprise that many fans of bands from the opposite end of this table loathe Bon Jovi for their lightweight riffing and crossover success, but this canny, populist band were never about to be Black Flag or Fugazi.

They know the value of a killer chorus and a stadium-filling anthem, and their only lyrical agenda is having a good time, all of the time. For which, you have to say, respect is grudgingly due.

MÖTLEY CRÜE

I should declare an interest here as the co-author of Mötley Crüe bassist Nikki Sixx's 2007 confessional autobiography, *The Heroin Diaries*. Joining his band on their arena-filling Carnival of Sins tour for weeks at a time helped me to grasp the appeal of this – to some ears – inexplicably popular US institution and rogue heavy-rock chemical element.

Mötley Crüe can easily be regarded as the most extreme, outré manifestation of the late-eighties glam metal scene that arose from Los Angeles's Sunset Strip, but band founder and songwriter Sixx grew up inspired not by the labyrinthine blues of Zeppelin but the flash, dash and fuck-you attitude of New York Dolls and the Sex Pistols: his all-time hero is Sid Vicious.

Easily one of this table's showier, more flammable elements, Mötley were always as concerned with statement and spectacle as with heads-down rock and roll: Sixx's early specialism was setting fire to himself in interviews, and to this day their live shows feature enough pyrotechnics to fuel a Michael Bay movie.

To their great credit and shame, Mötley took the cruder, lewder aspects of glam metal and ran with them: bawdy anthems like 'Girls, Girls, Girls' and 'Don't Go Away Mad (Just Go Away)' betray a certain unreconstructed attitude towards the fairer sex, as does drummer Tommy Lee's habit of brandishing a 'titty cam' during live shows to encourage perplexingly willing female fans to flash their breasts.

Furthermore, the band's jaw-dropping autobiography *The Dirt* confirmed that, whatever position they hold in this table, Mötley Crüe's determined consumption of chemicals over the years has been heroic.

RATT

Spectacularly of and for their time, Ratt were a group who achieved large-scale US success despite demonstrating no discernible originality, authenticity or, indeed, talent of any kind.

Their singer, Stephen Pearcy, had been around the block a few times and was already nearing 30 when they released their debut album, 1984's *Out Of The Cellar*, which was palpably in debt to bluesy and heavy-rock titans of the time such as Aerosmith and Van Halen.

But Ratt were just the sort of thing that a fledgling MTV were going for, and they duly did, sending the album multi-platinum and giving the band a platform for interchangeable videos of pouting LA wannabe models and actresses in advanced states of undress.

It was a slam-dunk: Ratt's functional fusing of glam-rock riffs, soft-porn visuals and fuck-you attitude saw them join Guns N' Roses, Mötley Crüe, Bon Jovi and Poison at hair metal's late 1980s top table.

Yet like many of these peacock bands, chemicals were to be Ratt's undoing, as their guitarist Robbin Crosby (who once shared an LA apartment with Mötley Crüe's Nikki Sixx: fuck knows how the housework ever got done) succumbed to heroin and cocaine addiction, which made his musical contributions increasingly erratic: he was eventually to die of an overdose in 2002.

Ratt have split and re-formed countless times, and a version of the band is still limping on; they remain one of hard rock's more unedifying alloys.

POISON

The study of elements and compounds, chemistry is an exact science that, when applied to the world of rock, becomes a roulette.

Juxtaposing apparently similar, complementary elements can occasion a highly negative reaction. You might imagine that the molecular compositions of 1980s glam-rock goliaths Poison and Mötley Crüe were virtually identical, but were these dirty compounds to happen across each other at an awards show, TV studio or brothel, violent and damaging explosions would inevitably ensue.

Maybe their chemical make-up was just too similar: moving from their native Pennsylvania in the mid-eighties, Poison aped the Crüe by plying their trade on the Sunset Strip circuit and mimicked their shock-metal, sleazy, innuendo-laden aesthetic on their early albums *Look What The Cat Dragged In* and *Open Up And Say... Ahh!*

Poison's musical elements were not rocket science: screeching punk-metal riffs, lewd lyrical come-ons and a bubblegum-pop sensibility that seduced MTV to fire them up the Billboard charts (although, like Mötley Crüe, they never really replicated this success in Britain: maybe some things are just *too* American).

Their shtick was tacky excess and they revelled in it: singer Bret Michaels even took the band's laboratory reproduction of Mötley Crüe to an absurdist degree by, like Tommy Lee, filming a sex tape with Pamela Anderson.

Indeed, switching from chemistry to the realm of human biology, Poison's sexual adventuring was legendary, with one notorious 1990s US jaunt featuring a tour bus on which fans eager to pleasure the band were given their own waiting room, complete with a condom machine (own coins required). Classy.

W.A.S.P.

As soon as they named their debut single 'Animal (Fuck Like A Beast)', W.A.S.P. established themselves as one of the more rudimentary elements in this table.

The Los Angeles band were uncharacteristically tight-lipped on the meaning of their acronymic name: the smart money was on White Anglo-Saxon Protestants, but scratched into the vinyl of their eponymous 1984 debut album was the legend 'We Are Sexual Perverts'.

Led by opportunistic, motormouth singer and bassist Blackie Lawless, W.A.S.P. set about making good on this claim with a live show that borrowed heavily on the riffs and costumes of Kiss and the debauched theatricality of Alice Cooper. Semi-naked women were manacled to onstage 'torture racks'; raw meat was hurled into audiences.

It was heavy rock, sure, but it also smacked of metal pantomime, and consequently W.A.S.P. had a distinct problem getting anybody to take them seriously.

Lawless's men also came up against a far more terrifying abbreviation in the PMRC (Parents' Music Resource Center), the puritanical Washington committee led by Tipper Gore who pursued them for what they regarded as their sexist and offensive material.

Yet in truth controversies such as this aided W.A.S.P.: their real problems began when the carefully manufactured aura of scandal and outrage that initially surrounded them faded, and rock fans realised that their *très ordinaire* music was really not much cop.

As their record sales slumped at the back end of the 1980s, W.A.S.P. split by the end of the decade, although like a pantomime dame unwilling to leave the stage, Lawless has assembled lesser line-ups under the same name ever since.

SPINAL TAP

Heavy rock can be a profoundly vainglorious affair. So many monstrous egos in daft hairdos and too-tight trousers, striving to roll the world into a question via the medium of portentous concept albums and thrusting guitar solos... what could possibly go wrong?

Immortalised in Rob Reiner's classic 1984 movie *This Is Spinal Tap*, Spinal Tap are the low comedy and banality of self-important heavy rock laid bare. Getting lost in venue corridors en route to the stage, losing drummers to bizarre gardening accidents and spontaneous combustion, writing a preposterous 'Jazz Odyssey' and a semi-classical piece called 'Lick My Love Pump', lauding amps that 'go up to 11' and accidentally ordering an 18-inch rather than 18-foot stage-prop replica of Stonehenge, the Tap are a salutary reprimand to every heavy-rock group in history whose creative ambitions have dwarfed their abilities and their intelligence.

Everything that can possibly go wrong for Spinal Tap does so, from suffering the indignity of being billed beneath a puppet show to hosting fan-free autograph signing sessions for their album *Smell The Glove*, to seeing the album banned for its sexist cover ('What's wrong with being sexy?'), yet they lurch on regardless, their faith in their risibly over-ambitious endeavours as absolute as was Rick Wakeman's when he staged *King Arthur on Ice*.

This Is Spinal Tap's lancing of rock's serial idiocies and absurdities was so sharp and forensic that it is unlikely there is one band in this Periodic Table who did not wince in recognition when they first saw it. Especially the ones who are currently residing in the 'Where are they now?' file...

STEEL PANTHER

88	09
Se	
Steel Panther	

Science and satire may appear unlikely bedmates, but – whisper it soft – many of the artists making up this Periodic Table are ripe for parody.

Spinal Tap remain the original and the best, but Steel Panther are making a very decent fist of ridiculing the peccadilloes and pretensions of 1980s hair metal at its most preposterous and priapic. Their underlying message is this: like, how did anybody ever take these dudes seriously?

It is telling that this forensically accurate spoof heavy-metal band began life as a turn-of-the-millennium in-joke in the clubs of Sunset Strip before support slots with the very bands they were parodying – Guns N' Roses, Mötley Crüe, a whole tour with Judas Priest – lifted them to the point where they can now sell out Wembley Arena.

Visually, Steel Panther's stage is an orgy of leather, Spandex, scarves and wind machines turned up to 11, while musically they sound every bit as proficient as the poodle rockers they are ridiculing, despite bassist Lexxi Foxx spending much of the night primping his luscious locks in a full-length mirror.

Lyrically, songs like 'Death To All But Metal' brilliantly nail the blinkered aesthetics of hard rock's most fervent adherents, while they have also imported the casual sexism and misogyny of eighties metal wholesale:

sleazeball tracks such as 'Fat Girl (Thar She Blows)'
and 'Asian Hooker' need little by way of explanatory
footnotes.

What does it say of human nature, then, that scores
of female fans at their gigs are as desperate to flash their
breasts on the venues' big screens as are the subjects of
Tommy Lee's titty cam? I only wish I knew.

Base
Metals

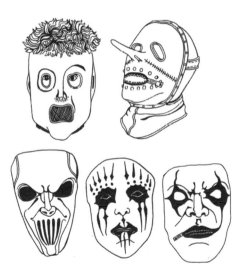

It's entirely fitting that the most diehard, fundamentalist metalloids are corralled in this subsection at the bottom of the Periodic Table, sectioned away from its main body.

For many years, heavy metal endured a pariah status in the music world, the unhappy recipient of much snobbery from fans of other, purportedly more rarefied genres who tended to regard metal as stunted music for troglodytes: *there dwell monsters.*

It was a vicious circle: this disdain bred a siege mentality in both the artists and their followers, which led to metal becoming ever more entrenched. Yet attitudes have shifted, minds have opened, and metal is no longer ghettoised. No one bats an eyelid when Metallica headline Glastonbury.

These final ferrous compounds are dived by row into two subsections: base metals ancient and modern.

Ancient

The names reek of Tommy Vance *Friday Night Rock Show* sessions from back in the mists of time. They conjure up 40-date tours that took in Stafford Bingley Hall and always, *always,* finished at London Hammersmith Odeon.

Between them, these 15 acts have been head-banging for more than 500 years.

AC/DC

AC/DC may be the basest of metals, but this does not mean that they are not precious.

As elemental as the outback and seemingly impervious to change, these Aussie rock colossi have shifted more than 200 million albums over the last four decades by the brutally effective means of stripping heavy metal down to its very essence.

Tellingly, they began as an extreme chemical reaction: when guitarist brothers Malcolm and Angus Young launched the band in Sydney in 1973, the rock world was dominated by the theatrical and overbearing symphonies of Britain's prog-rock behemoths.

AC/DC could not have rejected these excesses more totally or decisively. Their debut album, 1975's *High Voltage*, set the tenor and the parameters for what was to follow for the next 40 years: pulverising pared-down blues metal, brutal riffs like short-arm jabs to the solar plexus, and lewd, sleazy lyrics whose destiny it was to be scrawled on school-playground walls across the globe.

AC/DC shrewdly appeal to the acne-ridden, snickering adolescent in all of us: it is more of a metaphor than a gimmick that Angus Young has spent his entire career performing in short trousers and a school uniform, and continues to do so as he nears 70.

And fittingly for a band so rooted in arrested development, AC/DC have never exhibited the slightest interest in trying to mature or develop: there is not a Rizla paper between, say, 'TNT' from 1975 and 'Big Jack' from 2008's *Black Ice*.

They survived the 1980 alcohol-related death of their founding singer Bon Scott, replacing him with Geordie Brian Johnson and his sandpaper yowl, and are head-banging on even with Malcolm Young having left the band suffering from dementia, and drummer Phil Rudd currently facing serious police charges. Some chemical elements are simply indestructible.

MOTÖRHEAD

Were you to scratch away every extraneous or superfluous feature from heavy rock, the rough matter that remained would be Motörhead.

Much like their Antipodean kinsmen AC/DC, they have carved out a 40-year (and rising) career by being entirely rudimentary and reductionist – and, of course, very, very loud. It's take-it-or-leave-it hard rock with zero aesthetic or transformative ambition: metal that never rusts or, indeed, experiences any changes whatsoever.

Band founder, singer, bassist and talisman Lemmy first appeared in 1970s space cadets Hawkwind, but having been fired after a Canadian drug arrest, quickly decided that he wanted nowt more to do with cosmic prog-rock bollocks, instead founding a power trio that he intended to call Bastard.

Persuaded that this might jeopardise radio play, he settled on Motörhead and set about blasting out a frill-free strain of adrenalin- (and amphetamine-) driven hard rock that fused the volume and mass of metal with the speed and fuck-you attitude of punk.

It is a simple formula and Motörhead have stuck to it and stuck at it, making a virtue of their lack of frills and finesse, adhering to their fundamentalist rock mantra like raddled evangelists in biker jackets (items that are as mandatory at their gigs as ear plugs).

To some ears they have always sounded like old vinyl Black Sabbath albums played at 45rpm, but while Motörhead are easily mocked – they even do it themselves – they are also much loved and massively influential, being credited in many quarters with the *de facto* invention of speed metal. Their commercial apex came in 1981 when live album *No Sleep 'Til Hammersmith* went to number 1 in the UK.

Lemmy has never gone out of fashion – largely due to the fact that he has never been in it in the first place.

SCORPIONS

91	72
Sc	
Scorpions	

The vast majority of globally successful hard-rock and heavy-metal bands have been British or American, and a school of thought holds that an Anglo-Saxon sensibility is required to produce one particular piquant mix of testosterone, bad poetry and lewd sexism. The Scorpions proved that middle Europeans, and specifically Germans, can be equally prone to such debilitating failings.

Forming in Hanover in 1969, vocalist Rudolf Schenker recruited his young brother Michael to play guitar, only for him promptly to be nicked by Brit rockers UFO. Scorpions then churned out a series of fair-to-mediocre mid-1970s albums that lay within the emerging melodic heavy-metal movement without adding anything remotely new to it.

Meanwhile the younger Schenker was being defenestrated from UFO for his hard-partying habits, and returned to Scorpions in time for 1979 album *Lovedrive*. The record's cover image of a suit-wearing businessman pulling bubblegum from a woman's naked breast in the back of a car fuelled nocturnal fantasies for adolescent metal fans across the globe but did the band few favours in America, where, in true Spinal Tap style, it was banned for obscenity.

Their wayward guitarist then exited again to form the pop-metal Michael Schenker Group and his brother and Scorpions simply soldiered on. They hit paydirt with 'Wind Of Change', which became the unofficial anthem of the fall of the Berlin Wall as well as Germany's best-selling song ever, but the band then fell out of favour during the grunge revolution.

Around the millennium, the Scorpions toyed with techno and with orchestras, which fooled nobody at all: they are, and will forever be, workmanlike hard rockers.

RAINBOW

A base metal they may be, but Rainbow got together with distinctly rarefied aims.

Bored with the dumbed-down direction of Deep Purple, the band who once recorded the painfully ambitious *Concerto For Group and Orchestra*, Purple founder and guitarist Ritchie Blackmore quit the band in 1975 to start afresh.

Recruiting dramatic, operatic Italian-American vocalist Ronnie James Dio, he formed Rainbow and melded crunching, uncompromising riffs to the kind of dungeons-and-dragons lyrical medieval fantasies that led to not-very-bright schoolboys sketching swords and serpents on their school exercise books.

Blackmore and Dio piloted this formula through three moderately successful albums, but the chemistry between the band's notably egotistical partners was flawed, and Dio flounced off in 1979 to replace Ozzy Osbourne in Black Sabbath.

The jilted Blackmore then recalibrated the band, jettisoning Dio's there-dwell-dragons lyrical fixations and bringing in new singer Graham Bonnet to give Rainbow a far more businesslike hard-rock direction. This yielded raucous, bluesy sing-a-long hits like 'Since You've Been Gone' but album sales fell away and it was bye-bye Bonnet, as Blackmore recruited US vocalist Joe Lynn Turner.

Yet their first album together, 1981's *Difficult to Cure*, was a strange and schizophrenic beast, opening with the radio-friendly roustabout of pop-metal single 'I Surrender', and closing with a six-minute faux-classical piece based on Beethoven's Ninth Symphony.

Confused, much? The listeners certainly were, and as hard-rock fans turned to the bands spearheading the emerging New Wave of British Heavy Metal and Rainbow's album sales slowly dwindled, Blackmore gave up the ghost in 1984 and headed back for the mother ship of a re-formed Deep Purple.

Rainbow had helped him enjoy a chemical after-life of sorts – but he never quite decided what kind of compound they were.

DIO

Chemistry, biology and natural selection might suggest that a strutting rock god would invariably be strapping, hirsute and built like Thor.

Not so. Italian-American vocalist Ronnie James Dio stood a mere five foot four in his socks and, as his locks receded, looked increasingly like a hard-rocking Max Wall, and yet fronted not one but three major-league heavy-rock goliaths.

He brought to each of them a fine set of throbbing, operatic, vibrato-heavy, heavy-metal pipes, and a lyrical fixation with swords, sorcery and diabolic intervention that was easily mocked but also hugely emulated. To that extent, he was a polarising figure, epitomising what so many found plain daft about metal, yet bringing fantastical thrills and escapism to millions.

Dio was never short of employers: Ritchie Blackmore head-hunted him from his first band Elf to front Rainbow, Dio then moved on to replace a tired and emotional Ozzy Osbourne in Black Sabbath. It says much for Dio that even supplanting an iconic, much-loved figure like Ozzy, he was immediately accepted by Sabs fans.

Tiring of battling with Sabbath guitarist Tony Iommi, he left in 1982 to form his own band, which gave him the chance to indulge his angels 'n' devils lyrical worldview to his heart's content – his best-selling album, 1984's *The Last In Line*, carried a cover image like a Marvel comic's vision of hell.

Dio continued to throw out undeniably hard-rocking and likeably daft albums called things like *Lock Up The Wolves*, *Killing The Dragon* and *Master Of The Moon* but his appeal was growing decidedly more selective – or maybe Internet-weaned kids just got rather more sophisticated.

Metal's most diminutive deity died of throat cancer in Texas in 2010. He is also generally credited with having invented the throwing of devil's horns at rock gigs. Now *there* is a legacy.

WHITESNAKE

Actually, maybe it was somewhat harsh to describe this table's previous entry, Ronnie James Dio, as a polarising element – at least most rock fans like him.

If you truly want a divisive figure, look no further than David Coverdale. For each metaller who thinks him a strutting, leonine rock god, another finds him a preposterous poltroon and pretender.

Coverdale passed muster as the singer of late-period Deep Purple but began attracting decidedly mixed notices when he formed his own band, Whitesnake. Traditional heavy-metal fans have a high tolerance threshold – puzzlingly, an actual affection – for twiddly-widdly guitar solos, am-dram videos, chauvinistic guff and wailing men in leopard-skin trousers, but Whitesnake pushed even these aficionados to the limit.

There is a thin dividing line between rock grandeur and Spandex-clad self-parody, and Whitesnake teetered along it. That said, although more macho metal fans often viewed Coverdale as a narcissistic fake, the people who liked him *really* liked him: in their halcyon days of the 1980s, when hairspray metal ruled the roost, the 'Snake saw six consecutive albums go top 10 in the UK and even enjoyed hit singles with the likes of 'Here I Go Again' and 'Is This Love', and saw their eponymous 1987 album go a jaw-dropping eight times platinum in the US.

The truth is that David Coverdale is an intelligent man and, like all of the best glam metallers, he was always in on the joke: how else do you write songs with titles like 'Slow Poke Music'? Whitesnake are here, among the base metals, because they tick every cliché in the heavy-metal handbook: what redeems them, and ultimately earns Coverdale his pass from ridicule, is that they are *fun*.

95   75

Tn
Ted Nugent

TED NUGENT

Science is universal and chemistry does not recognise national borders but thankfully Britain never 'got' the gross, lumpen base metal that is Ted Nugent. This veteran guitar hero is an American institution, but there again, so is the Confederate flag.

In the early 1960s, Nugent wielded a heavy, psychedelic axe in gonzo Detroit band the Amboy Dukes, appearing alongside those other local counter-culture sensations the MC5 and the Stooges, and earning himself the nickname the Motor City Madman: not a bad achievement when you're up against Iggy Pop.

Going solo in the 1970s, Nugent switched to a more straightforward, ornery strain of hard rock, belching out endless belligerent blues-metal numbers that virtually accused you of looking at their pint and offered you outside.

These naturally played well in the Deep South and Midwest, as indeed did Nugent's personal views: from the 1980s on, he became known as much for his right-wing libertarian, pro-shooting, pro-hunting opinions as for his music, becoming a *bête noire* among heavy rock's few more liberal followers.

Yet the contrary Nugent is a mass of contradictions: despite his good-ol'-boy worldview, he is teetotal and has never touched drugs, a lifestyle that was an influence on US hardcore's late 1980s straight-edge bands (although his political standpoints more certainly were not).

As for his sexual politics, the fact he has released albums called *Penetrator*, *Little Miss Dangerous* and *If You Can't Lick 'Em... Lick 'Em* probably tells you all that you need to know. Or, if you are still in doubt, flick through the pages of his 2002 autobiography, *God, Guns & Rock 'n' Roll*.

A base metal Ted Nugent most certainly is, but this doesn't stop him being both acidic and gaseous.

VAN HALEN

Who was the crazed rock scientist who invented the widdly-widdly guitar solo, the bizarre six-string aggregation of effects and semitones that seems to last forever? (Exempted from this charge are the profound, impassioned gymnastics of Jimi Hendrix, who really did feel as if he were touching the sky: accused is the showy, look-at-me slick virtuosity that gives so much metal a bad name.)

Prime suspect: Eddie Van Halen, a man who will never play one note where ten will do. His molten guitar arabesques and improvisations frequently sound as if he is tying knots in his strings, and as if he considerers this to be a good thing.

Obsessed by Eric Clapton's playing in Cream, which he would slow down to 16rpm to analyse, Eddie Van Halen formed the band that narcissistically bears his name in 1973, with his older brother Alex on drums, and a flaxen-haired would-be rock god named David Lee Roth as singer. A pouting coxcomb, Roth was an exemplary metal vocalist, but the band was always about Van Halen Jr's extraordinary touch and technique.

Through the late 1970s into the early 1980s their nimble, canny pop-metal albums regularly went top 10 in the US, but after 'Jump' became their biggest hit and first number 1 single in 1985, Eddie and Roth could no longer bear to be around each other and Roth flounced off. It was business as usual after Eddie recruited new singer Sammy Hagar – in fact, it improved as Van Halen's next four US albums hit number 1, at which point Eddie promptly defenestrated Hagar.

A third singer, Gary Cherone, was to be short-lived, and Roth was to return to the fold – but as Eddie Van Halen knew full well, the band were always about his right hand. And you have to respect a man who, legend has it, did not enjoy *This Is Spinal Tap* because, to him, it seemed too much like a documentary.

JUDAS PRIEST

AC/DC and Motörhead may be the bands who distilled heavy metal to its raw essence in the 1970s but another compound coalesced at the same time was equally influential.

Having formed in 1970, West Midlands rockers Judas Priest spent most of the decade building their name and honing their piledriving, power-chord-heavy rock assault, pausing for occasional diversions into ballads or gothic prog rock. Those latter features had been entirely eschewed from their repertoire by 1978, when the blistering album *Stained Class* established them firmly at the head of the UK music press's much vaunted New Wave of British Heavy Metal, alongside Iron Maiden, Def Leppard and Saxon (as well as Dumpy's Rusty Nuts, of whom we hear so little nowadays).

The NWOBHM was contrived to give a boost to British metal in the face of the perceived decline of veteran hard-hitters such as Black Sabbath and Deep Purple, and in many ways Priest were worthy successors to those bands, incorporating their looming air of doom into eviscerating, streamlined numbers that hit harder, deeper, faster.

They had barbed angst aplenty – indeed, their Spooky Tooth cover, 'Better By You, Better Than Me' landed them before America's preposterous Parents Music Resource Center, accused of infiltrating backward messages among their riffs, urging fans to kill themselves. The lugubrious Rob Halford commented in court that were Priest to place subliminal messages in their songs, they would be more likely to say, 'Buy more of our records'.

Their fans have continued to do just that: more than 40 years after their debut, Judas Priest have sold 50 million records worldwide, with 2014's *Redeemer Of Souls* becoming their first US Billboard chart top 10 hit.

Better yet, when Rob Halford came out as gay in 1998, the metal world was entirely supportive – an unthinkable outcome when this gnarly band of survivors formed back in the distant, dark 1970s.

IRON MAIDEN

Given that heavy metal is so predicated on transgression and on being wild rock-and-roll outlaws living outside of society – is it possible for a metal band to become national treasures?

Whether they like it or not, that fate has largely befallen Iron Maiden. A group who started off being heralded as radical and ground-breaking for the way they took the basic metal template and twisted everything – sound, volume, power – up a notch are now largely perceived as, well, cuddly. You can imagine them on ITV1 on a weekend night, maybe at a Royal Variety Show or guest-drawing the lottery numbers.

This is not to imply any limp sell-out on their part: in truth, Iron Maiden have just carried on doing what they do, over a 40-year career that has seen them record 15 studio albums and sell close on 90 million records. Probably that is the point: the longevity has bred a familiarity that has grown not into contempt but benign affection.

Bruce Dickinson has yet to film a TV reality show where he pads bemusedly around his kitchen while his kids laugh at him, Ozzy-style, but the transition has been similar. Like Ozzy, he has grown into a character outside of his hard-rocking day job, an English eccentric flying airplanes, fencing against Olympians and writing a comedy novel called *The Adventures of Lord Iffy Boatrace*. Plus, of course, the band's supposedly fearsome mascot Eddie always looked like he belonged in *2000 AD* alongside Judge Dredd.

When Dickinson announced he was fighting cancer of the tongue in 2015, it elicited a wave of national sympathy as if the news had been announced by Cilla Black or Lionel Blair. Bruce Dickinson has learned a skill beyond so many heavy rockers who succumb to misguided chemical experiments or go up in flames: he is growing old gracefully.

DEF LEPPARD

If Iron Maiden are UK heavy metal's national treasures, Def Leppard are its local boys made good, overcoming a host of hurdles and setbacks along the way.

From the stone denim to the fluffed hairdos, there has always been something inescapably provincial about them; even when they were topping both the UK and US album charts in the late 1980s and early 1990s they always appeared plucky underdogs.

No matter how many million albums they shift or at how many stadiums Joe Elliott asks, 'How ya doin'?', Leppard always seem to be slightly sniggery, superannuated schoolboys writing songs like 'Pour Some Sugar On Me' and 'Let's Get Rocked' *just because they can*.

The general affection felt for them both in metal and non-metal circles has its roots in that underdog status, their humble Sheffield beginnings (unlike most metal singers, Elliott was a glam-rock buff, adoring both Bowie and Mott the Hoople) and a knack for overcoming adversity, most famously when drummer Rick Allen lost an arm in a car accident on New Year's Eve 1984. Rather than jettisoning him, Def Leppard stuck by their stricken colleague as he learned how to use a specially customised drum kit that allowed him to trigger the hi-hat with a foot pedal.

Allen's accident happened at the height of Leppard's salad days, when two streamlined, super-slick pop-metal albums with arena-friendly choruses, *Pyromania* (1983) and *Hysteria* (1987), both went multi-multi platinum in America. In recent years Def Leppard have subsisted at a still huge but no longer stellar level, and the reliably level-headed Elliott has founded and fronted tribute bands to his teenage musical loves, Bowie and Mott.

100	79
Sa	
Saxon	

SAXON

Def Leppard may be easily pinned as loveable heavy-metal oiks who got lucky, but they are veritable rock sophisticates next to the figurative grunting troglodytes of Saxon.

Like Leppard, Judas Priest and Iron Maiden, Saxon were given a hefty leg-up towards fame and fortune by the 1979 New Wave of British Heavy Metal (MWOBHM) movement, but they never remotely equalled the success of their rivals. In hindsight, they probably had as much chance of becoming big in America as had shove ha'penny, *The Wheeltappers And Shunters Social Club* or Yorkshire pudding.

Born in Barnsley, fronted by a man called 'Biff' Byford and originally handing themselves the cute name Son of a Bitch, Saxon looked like rock dinosaurs even in their earliest days. Aiming fair and square for the biker market with songs like 'Motorcycle Man' and signature tune 'Wheels Of Steel', they released stodgy, meat-and-potatoes albums with titles like *Denim and Leather* and *Power & The Glory*, and slogged up and down the M1 and M6 supporting Motörhead.

This strategy worked, in as much as they garnered a loyal head-banging fan base, mainly in the North and Midlands, and were able to play as many Tommy Vance-hosted *Friday Rock Show* sessions as any sane person could take, but unlike their peers there was never any hint of any crossover success. Saxon were just too unreconstructed, their metal too base and bellicose.

Biff and his lads all looked like mechanics, their riffs chugged along like an old Ford Cortina rather than a silver machine to hell, and the glamour-obsessed MTV gave them a very wide berth. By 1984 Saxon were even writing a concept album about great conquests in history, *Crusader*, which really wasn't them at all.

Thirty years later, they are still banging along... well, of course they are. It's the only thing they know.

101 82
Ma
Manowar

MANOWAR

Brash, boorish Saxon make up one kind of very silly heavy metal band. Brash, boorish Manowar comprise another, and are far more unwittingly entertaining.

These veteran New York heavy rockers take to the extreme a school of raw yet overblown, preposterous faux-noble metal that appears to regret that the days of the reign of Zeus, or at least the court of King Arthur, are behind us.

Behind them, like a string of droppings, lie 30 years' worth of ludicrous albums called things like *Battle Hymns*, *Sign Of The Hammer* and *Gods Of War*. They all lie within covers that can best be summarised as Thor The God Of Thunder Goes For The Pink Pound. Buffed and Photoshopped to within an inch of their lives, the band members stand naked except for fur underpants or chaps, meaningfully waving scimitars. Their alternative sleeves feature graphic cartoons of warrior gods who clearly breakfast on steroids, sometimes cheerfully brandishing severed heads.

Manowar's 1984 opus *Hail To England* featured a cover of a pumped, raging god in eagle headwear clutching a bloodied sword and a Union Jack, and tracks such as 'Blood Of My Enemies' and 'Kill With Power'. Nice try, lads, but England reacted with snorts of derisive laughter and an album-chart placing of number 83: indeed, given their predilection for Viking chic, it is no surprise that Manowar's most fervent international market is Sweden.

These intrepid guitar-wielding warriors don't just fart out relentless stentorian twaddle; they do as at an unbearable volume, being cited in *The Guinness Book of Records* as the world's loudest band, having scaled 129 decibels in 1994 in Hamburg. To ram this point home, in 2014 they re-released their 'classic' 1988 album, *Kings Of Metal*, with a spoken narration by Brian Blessed. You don't catch Metallica doing stuff like that.

102	88
Gw	
GWAR	

GWAR

GWAR! What are they good for? Well, how about rampaging, bloodthirsty panto-metal?

Gazing over this Periodic Table, the unscientific eye may fail to see much difference between the band whose acronymic name (allegedly) stands for God What An Awful Racket and Manowar, but that eye would be blind. The two groups are equally preposterous, but GWAR's stupidity is wholly intentional.

Formed in 1988 by students and musicians at Virginia Commonwealth University, the group purported to be carnal invading aliens hell-bent on reducing Earth to rubble, and awarded themselves monikers such as Oderus Urungus (vocals) and Beefcake the Mighty (bass).

Albums such as *Scumdogs Of The Universe* (1990) and *This Toilet Earth* (1994) boasted songs like 'Saddam A Go-Go' that were rarely as entertaining as their titles and were largely of secondary importance to the group's live gigs. This orgiastic vaudeville show sees GWAR, in latex and monster costumes, act out pagan rituals, spew fake blood and bodily fluids over the crowd, battle dinosaurs, decapitate George W. Bush, the Pope and Justin Bieber and, most grisly of all, cover Billy Ocean's 'Get Outta My Dreams, Get Into My Car'.

GWAR have never broken through to the mainstream and mansion-purchasing levels of success as did their spiritual grandfather, Alice Cooper, but it's hard not to think that Slipknot were paying their aesthetic and business model some seriously close attention.

They sought outrage and they got it, with various shows in America's Bible Belt banned or cut short over the years, but have spasmodically flirted with respectability: they even got nominated for a Grammy for their 1992 band movie *Phallus In Wonderland*. Sadly, the carnal invading aliens hell-bent on reducing Earth to rubble lost, to Annie Lennox.

103	81
Av	
Anvil	

ANVIL

The Periodic Table has its obscure elements and heavy rock has its unsung heroes; bands who stood on the brink of fame and global success, then toppled headlong into the abyss of anonymity.

Canadian metallers Anvil are the most poignant nearly men of all. Speed-metal pioneers, their star rose rapidly in the early 1980s: at 1984's Super Rock festival in Japan, the headliners were Whitesnake, Scorpions, Bon Jovi and Anvil.

Thereafter… nothing. Record label woes, a dodgy album or two and tastes simply moving on relegated them to two decades as also-rans, putting out albums that barely registered even in Canada.

Yet in 2005 a British former Anvil roadie turned successful screenwriter, Sacha Gervasi, made a documentary about them. *Anvil! The Story of Anvil* captured the bathos and sense of absurdity that so often envelops heavy metal.

Invited by a female Swiss-Italian fan to play a comeback European tour, Anvil arrived in Europe high on hope only to miss trains, get lost in Prague, bicker with promoters, play to near-empty venues and, penniless, sleep in train stations. At the Monsters of Transylvania festival in a 10,000-seat arena, only 174 people turned up. Returning to Canada, one of the band found himself homeless; another married the eccentric Swiss-Italian fan, and Anvil played at their wedding reception.

The similarities to Spinal Tap are eerie, even to the degree that Anvil's drummer is called Robb Reiner, as was *This Is Spinal Tap*'s director, yet Anvil are a living, breathing band, one who were once even viewed as ground-breaking: 'Everybody just ripped them off and left them for dead,' admits Slash in the (very moving) movie.

Despite being constantly bashed in the face with the frying pan of fate, Anvil remain inveterate optimists, ending the film taking the stage as the opening act of the same Japanese festival they had headlined 20 years earlier.

Modern

Even as late as the early eighties, metal was still widely seen as the embarrassing relation of hipper, more inventive and original music, and was largely ostracised. But heavy rock, like research science, can make quantum leaps. Exiting the dungeons and slaying the dragons, some truly formidable, agenda-shifting bands emerged to reinvent the genre. Metal would never be the same.

METALLICA

The early 1980s saw a revolution in US metal that was as transformative as had been the punk explosion in Britain a few years earlier. Inspired by the ferocity of hardcore and the back-to-basics thrust of New Wave of British Heavy Metal groups like Motörhead and Judas Priest, a quartet of single-minded American bands honed thrash metal to a brutal, gleaming point. Metallica were the apex of this movement.

Their mechanistic and yet febrile and very human music seemed to have more in common with an advanced branch of mathematics than it did with chemistry, intertwining intricate dual-guitar riffs, squealing solos and tumultuous double-bass drumming into eerily malevolent, frequently episodic metal symphonies.

It was a rebirth for heavy rock, and it felt like a whole new kind of simultaneously primal and futuristic music, shorn of all of old-school metal's frequent nonsensical referencing of swords, sorcerers or dragons. Instead, Metallica's intelligent caveman James Hetfield sang, in the most haunted, guttural of growls, of paranoia, societal dysfunction, mental illness and corrupt authorities: modern subject matters for a sleek yet labyrinthine music rooted firmly in the now.

Founding guitar Dave Mustaine had already been kicked out for alleged addiction issues by 1983's *Kill 'Em*

All debut, and as Metallica's fame, stature and influence grew exponentially over the next decade, they reacted by focusing ever more intensely and obsessively inwards, on their bleak, driven, increasingly epic music, until they appeared to be so tight and autonomous that they were hermetically sealed. Lauding a masterpiece such as 'Enter Sandman' felt like applauding a high-tensile piece of industrial machinery.

Yet Metallica were very human: witness their damaging legal battles with Napster over digital piracy, and the individual and group psychological breakdowns detailed in the bizarre and gripping *Some Kind Of Monster* documentary.

More than anything, Metallica showed that brooding, uncompromising heavy metal could also be high art. It was some achievement.

MEGADETH

One school of thought holds that Megadeth are the band that Metallica could have been. It is possible that Dave Mustaine is the only student in that school.

After Mustaine was kicked out of Metallica in 1983, he quickly formed Megadeth, a thrash-metal quartet that cleaved extremely precisely to his former band's musical template. Indeed, on their first two albums, 1985's *Killing Is My Business... And Business Is Good* and 1986's *Peace Sells... But Who's Buying?*, the similarities far outweighed any differences, not least because of material that Metallica originally conceived with Mustaine still in the band.

Yet the personal issues that had led to Mustaine being ejected from Metallica were also to hamper Megadeth. With the singer in the grip of heroin addiction, the *So Far, So Good... So What!* album sounded perfunctory and thrown together, not least with its cover of the Sex Pistols' 'Anarchy In The UK' with its misheard lyrics ('I want to destroy, possibly!' being the undoubted winner).

After a drink-driving conviction, Mustaine vanished into rehab and emerged a stronger and sober man but also one with a noted propensity for firing his fellow band members at a moment's notice. Where Metallica remained an integrated, band-of-brothers unit, surviving even the death in a road accident of original bassist Cliff Burton, Megadeth became essentially Dave Mustaine and whoever else was around, which meant they rarely achieved the holistic, ultra-tight intuitive rapport of their rivals.

Metallica and Megadeth were to bury the hatchet, sharing festival bills and even tours, and Mustaine's band were commercially successful, seeing six consecutive albums go platinum in the US. Yet next to Metallica's preternatural efficiency they have always felt somewhat more erratic; a heavy base metal, yet never the heaviest.

ANTHRAX

As thrash metal became the defining, cleansing force in US heavy rock in the early 1980s, four bands in the vanguard of this brutalist movement became known as the Big Four. As Metallica and Megadeth simultaneously speeded up metal and scoured it to the bone on the West Coast, Anthrax were doing the same in New York City.

The musical template was remarkable similar: powerhouse guitarists Scott Ian and Dan Spitz mixed serpentine intertwined riffs with hell-for-leather solos that sounded necessary and urgent rather than superfluous accoutrements, while vocalist Joey Belladonna, in situ from the band's second album, 1985's *Spreading The Disease*, onwards, was a suitably guttural while still yowling presence.

While their noise assault was reliably pulverising, Anthrax were never so apocalyptically earnest as Metallica; they scattered humour and irony among their more socially conscious lyrical diatribes, with 1987's *Among The Living* album featuring 'I Am The Law', a tribute to *2000 AD* comics ultra-authoritarian law-enforcement officer, Judge Dredd.

Nor were Anthrax as autonomous and rigidly self-contained as Metallica: the early 1990s saw the group increasingly embrace the hip-hop scene, including touring with Public Enemy and covering their righteous 'Bring The Noise' as a collaboration with them. It was an audacious experiment that doubtless lost them a few hidebound followers, but won them many more.

Yet for all of their critical status and impeccable reputation, Anthrax never shifted remotely as many records as did Metallica or Megadeth, and as the decade progressed they lost their way, sacking Belladonna and replacing him with a more traditionalist, less idiosyncratic singer in John Bush.

By the millennium this once combustible group seemed to be mainly about anthology albums and play-the-hits package tours – although a Grammy-nominated album of new songs, 2011's *Worship Music*, indicated that their days as one of thrash metal's Big Four weren't quite over yet.

107	83
Sr	
Slayer	

SLAYER

Three members of the Big Four US thrash-metal progenitors of the early 1980s abandoned heavy metal's conventional ways and mores completely. The fourth took a rather less scorched-earth policy.

Slayer's brittle, rapid-fire riffs and thunderous drumming were just as all-obliterating as those of Metallica, Megadeth and Anthrax, but unlike their peers, they did not put childish things behind them. From their very first, nuclear-riffing days in California, their lyric sheet featured as many ridiculous apocalypse and Armageddon scenarios as did those of Dio or even Manowar, and for all of their pious denials, they frequently lurched across the line into full-on cartoon satanic imagery.

Their standout, third album, 1986's *Reign In Blood*, was less than 30 minutes of serrated speed-metal splatter movies with titles such as 'Necrophobic' and 'Altar Of

Sacrifice'; lyrically, for anybody over 14 years old it was utterly risible, yet musically its nihilistic thrash was totally free of sonic spare or waste.

For everybody scoffing at Slayer's puerile Book of Revelations worldview, plenty more were marvelling, open-mouthed: they were to spawn the whole sub-cult of death metal as the lugubrious like of Obituary, Morbid Angel and Cannibal Corpse thrashed eagerly in their wake.

By the time of 1994 US top 10 album *Divine Intervention*, Slayer had hit on a devil's horn- and Pentagram-heavy formula and weren't about to deviate from it, as luridly titled future offerings such as *Diabolus In Musica* (1998), *God Hates Us All* (2001) and *Christ Illusion* (2006) were to testify.

A footnote: On 22 June 2010, Metallica, Megadeth, Anthrax and Slayer played the Sonisphere festival in Bulgaria. Their performances were shown live in cinemas and caught on an album, *The Big 4: Live From Sofia, Bulgaria,* capturing the innovators 30 years down the line. There were bald spots and beer bellies aplenty – but they sounded as vital, and as revolutionary, as ever.

NAPALM DEATH

108   87
Na
Napalm
Death

When Slayer (plus accomplices like Venom and Celtic Frost) gave the world death metal, numerous subgenres – black metal, doom metal, grindcore – mutated and reproduced like bacteria in a chemical laboratory Petri dish. Few disciples carried the first flame in a stranger direction than Napalm Death.

Formed in Birmingham in 1982, they fused the high-velocity thrash and doom-laden worldview of Slayer with a social militancy inherited from crypto-punk bands like Crass and Conflict, then sprinkled in their own, magic ingredient – the 'songs' were incredibly short.

Their debut album, 1987's *Scum*, crammed 28 tracks into 33 minutes, all of which sounded like the world's angriest man undergoing a seizure/temper tantrum while throwing up into a cement mixer. The briefest number,

'You Suffer', lasted for four seconds (live, they could get it down to two).

The truly bizarre thing was that, within these surreally reductive limitations, Napalm Death had a lyrical agenda; their next record, 1988's *From Enslavement To Obliteration*, featured numbers called 'Social Sterility' and 'Cock-Rock Alienation', although their exact message was somewhat blurred by the fact that singer Lee Dorrian's bowels-of-hell rasp was utterly unintelligible.

Helped by the amused patronage of late-night BBC Radio 1 DJ John Peel, Napalm Death forged a following that ranged from diehards who hung on their every word (even when that word was usually *Whhheeeeaaarrgh!*) to more casual listeners who loved the comedic absurdity of it all. Yet the joke could only be told so many times, and in the 1990s Napalm Death developed/ experimented/sold out the kids by introducing tunes and melodies to their down-tuned racket, occasionally even stretching songs past the three-minute mark.

More than 30 years on, they are still vomming into that cement mixer. *Whhheeeeaaarrgh!*

CANNIBAL CORPSE

Metal lends itself to shock tactics more readily than any other music genre. If the founders of death metal, Slayer, really felt they were 'the most extreme band in the world', as they were pinned for a while, they were kidding themselves: they were just a training slope.

Followers like Cannibal Corpse took the torch and ran with it, replicating the sheer, finger-threading slash and Lucifer-gargling-boiling-gravel vocals and adding snuff-movie lyrical topics such as gang rape, mass mutilation, feeding on putrefying flesh and ritual disembowelment.

With album sleeves that appeared to be ripped straight from zombie B-movie posters, the New York thrashers defined themselves from the offset against any notion of nuance, subtlety, compromise or FM-radio play: their debut album, 1990's *Eaten Back To Life*, set out their comedic-repulsive agenda with songs like 'Edible Autopsy', 'Scattered Remains, Splattered Brains' and 'A Skull Full Of Maggots'.

They were just warming up: other gems dredged up from the ensemble's none-more-bleak imagination over the ensuing 25 years and 14 albums have included 'Meat Hook Sodomy', 'Stripped, Raped And Strangled' and, ever a crowd-pleasing favourite, 'Entrails Ripped From A Virgin's Cunt'.

It's reasonable to surmise that they have expended far more energy on this area of their operations than they have on developing their music, which has remained a stringently unremarkable, colon-vibrating, death-metal chug.

Cannibal Corpse's *raison d'être* is to horrify society's more easily outraged, kneejerk elements and, well, job done: their albums were banned from sale en masse in both Australia and Germany for a decade. The authorities apparently found something offensive in songs like 'Necropedophile' and 'Post Mortal Ejaculation'. Pussies.

CRADLE OF FILTH

The world of extreme metal is insular and hierarchical, and defined by fine divisions invisible to the eye of the casual outsider. To anybody not steeped in noisome heavy rock, the difference between the speed metal of Anthrax, the death metal of Cannibal Corpse and the chainsaw racket made by Cradle of Filth may appear infinitesimal; to its protagonists and diehard acolytes, it is a gaping chasm.

Founded in the Luciferian netherworld of Suffolk in 1991, Cradle of Filth are black metallers, taking their musical cues from Judas Priest, Slayer and the infamous Norwegian black-metal scene of the 1980s (of which more next). The band's unique selling point, beyond some deeply theatrical, Alice Cooper-hued live shows, is that they take this bleak, nihilistic template and add to it a gothic, poignantly poetic romanticism, lying at times nearer to the once indie-trendy Goth rock of Sisters of Mercy or Bauhaus than they are to Metallica.

Ironically, ludicrous as it may appear to non-believers, the black-metal scene is highly predicated on perceived authenticity, and Cradle of Filth have their haters who regard them as dilettantes and poseurs with an eye for the main chance and a willingness to soften their riffs and introduce melodies to appease the mainstream. Fairer-minded observers may feel that this is a harsh accusation to level against a troupe who have given the world such songs as 'Lord Abortion', 'Sodomy And Lust' and 'The Foetus Of A New Day Kicking'.

Ultimately, it calls to mind the *Monty Python's Life of Brian* schism between the People's Front of Judea and the Judean People's Front, or even an attempt to differentiate between two of the real-life Periodic Table's minor inert gasses: as far as 99.999 per cent of people are concerned, Cradle of Filth are more than metallic enough to be getting on with.

MAYHEM

Black Sabbath, Slayer, Cradle of Filth and Cannibal Corpse may sporadically look to invoke Lucifer and summon forth dark forces by the means of shredding their guitars, but no one seriously believes they are satanic or evil. It's a game, a metal convention, showbiz.

The same caveat does not apply to Mayhem, the infamous Norwegian black metallers with a real-life band history to leave Stephen King reeling. Formed in Oslo in 1984 and taking their name from a Venom song, 'Mayhem With Mercy', their live gigs became notorious for corpse-painted vocalist Per Yngve Ohlin (aka Dead)'s habit of cutting himself with hunting knives, and impaling pigs' and sheep's heads on spikes on the stage.

When Dead shot himself in the head in the band's house in 1991, guitarist Øystein Aarseth (aka Euronymous) celebrated his singer's suicide by wearing fragments of his skull as a necklace (not an option that Dave Grohl is thought to have pondered three years later).

Fiercely anti-Christian, Norway's black-metal bands had an unfortunate habit of burning down their local churches, and Mayhem hatched a plot to blow up Nidaros Cathedral in Trondheim, which was to appear on the cover of their debut album, *De Mysteriis Dom Sathanas*. This plan was overtaken by events prior to the record's release when Mayhem's bassist, Varg Vikernes (aka Count Grishnackh), murdered Euronymous by stabbing him 23 times, allegedly jealous of the guitarist's none-more-evil public image.

Opening with a tribute called 'Funeral Fog', *De Mysteriis Dom Sathanas* was dedicated to Euronymous, but with Vikernes locked up for 21 years, drummer Jan Axel Blomberg (aka Hellhammer) broke up the band. He re-formed them a year later and Mayhem have recorded and toured ever since: one black-metal fan suffered a fractured skull at a 2003 gig when a sheep's head that guitarist Blasphemer was sawing from its body flew into the crowd.

Frankly, it all makes GWAR look a tad tame.

RAMMSTEIN

Happily, some Euro-metal bands know how to embrace the genre's glory and absurdity without resorting to intra-band slaying and wearing the deceased singer's cranium as costume jewellery.

A German institution equally capable of filling arenas across Europe and America, Rammstein are a tremendous amalgam of feverish grindcore, bombastic power metal, progressive rock showiness and high camp, all delivered – as is utterly mandatory – with the straightest of faces.

Their records, as indebted to the industrial noise of Ministry and KMFDM as they are to Megadeth or Slayer, are excess-all-areas slabs of sonic mayhem delivered with Teutonic order and control, and a weather eye for the taboo: the band took their name from a 1988 German air-show disaster in which 70 people died, while their song 'Weiner Blut' tells the real-life story of Josef Fritzl, the Austrian who imprisoned his daughter as a sex slave for 24 years.

Live, though, is where Rammstein come into their own. Their arena extravaganzas are noted for their dementedly OTT use of pyrotechnics, with their growling bass-baritone singer Till Lindemann frequently performing while aflame from head to toe, and for their use of visual gimmicks, from outlandish costumes to surfing the crowd in a rubber dinghy to spurting them with fake (well, so you assume) semen from a giant penis cannon. Touring their 2001 album *Mutter*, which bore a cover of a photo of a dead foetus, Rammstein began the show by descending to the stage from a model of a huge womb, while wearing nappies.

Together for more than 20 years, their six-member line-up has never changed, a constancy that goes some way towards explaining why Rammstein are the only absurdist shock-horror heavy-metal terrorists, singing in German, able to sell out Wembley Arena and Madison Square Garden.

SLIPKNOT

Imagine this lot as the sum of a gross heavy-metal equation. If you were to add the bleak worldview of Black Sabbath to the kinetic thrash-metal riffs of Anthrax, then multiply the end result by GWAR's costumed melodrama, you would get Slipknot.

The Des Moines, Iowa nine-piece have always appeared fuelled by seemingly limitless supplies of raw, inchoate rage, generated by both their own humble Midwest backwater origins and a more general, adolescent ire at their inability to bend the wider world to their will.

That is before you add the element of ritualistic pantomime: Slipknot have always appeared in grotesque, sub-Tim Burton horror masks to conceal their identities, and were working identical orange jumpsuits way before Guantanamo Bay happened along.

Their albums and live gigs are both akin to thunderous, max-volume teenage temper tantrums: Slipknot's anger at the world may be sincerely felt but it is also hugely inarticulate, being vented largely in retarded-development outbursts such as the baleful, glowering 'People = Shit'.

Led by the band's founder, percussionist and strategist Shawn Crahan, a man better known by his onstage persona of Clown, Slipknot masterminded their unsettling beyond-the-pale early public image brilliantly by means of anarchic live shows that saw members urinate and defecate on stage, throw the resulting turds at each other and at the audience and, in the case of the late bassist Paul Gray (aka Pig), masturbate inside his overalls. Clown was prone to sniffing the rotting corpse of a dead crow in a jar before going onstage, to trigger himself to projectile vomit through his mask.

It sounds like a certifiable freak show destined for shadowy, Cannibal Corpse-like cult status, but Slipknot have crossed over big, and then some, with two US number 1 albums and their own Ozzfest-style heavy metal festival, Knotfest. The merchandise stalls there, regrettably, do not sell rotting crows in jars.

PANTERA

Some heavy-rock bands seem to arrive fully formed; many others take a while for their chemical molecules to click into place.

Texan band Pantera spent the 1980s releasing fairly lame hair metal, Van Halen and Kiss-indebted albums with titles like *Metal Magic* and *Power Metal*; guitarist 'Dimebag' Darrell Abbott even had Kiss's Ace Frehley tattooed on his chest.

They performed a spectacular volte-face at the end of the decade when they wised up rather late to the mechanistic power of Metallica, Anthrax *et al*, and also recruited a new singer in Phil Anselmo. Their 1990 album *Cowboys From Hell* showcased a baleful, bludgeoning new approach that saw them attack their instruments as if they bore them a serious grudge, while Dimebag eschewed his previous penchant for widdly-widdly guitar in favour of surgical, chuntering heavy riffing.

It broke Pantera in a way that nobody had seen coming, and 1992 follow-up *Vulgar Display Of Power* capitalised on their new-found gravitas and credibility while sounding beside itself with existential rage. By the time of 1994's *Far Beyond Driven*, Pantera were going straight into the Billboard chart at number 1, an extraordinary feat for an extreme metal band with a history of obscurity behind them – but all was not well in their camp.

Anselmo fell into heroin abuse and even survived an overdose just after the release of 1996's *The Great Southern Trendkill*, and after the artistically and commercially disappointing *Reinventing The Steel* (2000), Pantera broke up. Any hopes for a potential reunion came to an end on 8 December 2004, at a gig by Dimebag Darrell's new band, Damageplan, in Columbus, Ohio, when he and three other people were shot and killed by a crazed fan in the crowd.

TOOL

115	93
T	
Tool	

Heavy rock has always had, and always will have, its fervent detractors; people who hold that 'intelligent metal' is an oxymoron to rank alongside 'caring Conservatism' or 'great German comedians'. Such naysayers would be well advised to investigate Tool.

As beholden to the audacious, choppy art rock of Faith No More and Jane's Addiction as they were the adrenalin thrust of post-Metallica thrash, they found themselves able to appeal both to a traditional hard-rock audience and the Nirvana-loving grunge hipsters who would usually regard anything resembling conventional metal with snobbish distaste.

In a medium where too many bands were still obsessed with bringing down pestilence or invoking the apocalypse, Tool sounded measured, rational and curious, dismantling subjects such as organised religion or enforced sodomy in prison like op-ed authors even as their churning riffs and propulsive drums raged around them. Unlike, say, Slipknot there was no need to hand your brain in at the door.

Their second album, *Ænima*, ventured into the kind of dense, episodic terrain favoured by 1970s progressive rockers such as King Crimson or even Yes without sacrificing their sharp, visceral edge, yet it was 2001's *Lateralus* that was Tool's real magnum opus. Brilliantly expansive and elaborate and yet also powerfully direct, the majority of its 13 tracks weighed in at over six minutes yet wasted none of that time, while the 11-minute 'Reflection' lambasted the solipsism gripping America's alternative nation: 'Don't wanna be down here, feeding my narcissism.'

Lateralus rocketed into the US album chart at number 1 as did its follow-up, 2006's *10,000 Days*. It is now close on a decade since Tool released new product: unlike so many of this Periodic Table's entrants, there is the certainty that it will be worth waiting for.

KORN

When speed metal's Big Four reinvented heavy rock at the outset of the 1980s, they felt like a necessary cleansing; a year-zero laying waste of what had gone before. To say the very least, the nu-metal arrivistes at the arse-end of the twentieth century seemed rather less essential.

Earnestly striving to infiltrate hip-hop and funk tropes into the insatiable rush of extreme metal, bands such as Limp Bizkit, Linkin Park and Papa Roach rarely became any more that the sum of their (arguably) well-intentioned but ultimately derivative parts.

At the risk of invoking tallest-dwarf syndrome, Korn were the best of the bunch. As angst-ridden as was *de rigueur* in the post-grunge years and honing their intemperate thrash with rap and art-rock rhythms, their second album, 1996's *Life Is Peachy*, was a US top 3 hit and smoothed the way for their creative and commercial zenith, 1998's *Follow The Leader*.

Sounding troubled and cathartic where too many of their peers were synthetic and calculating, the record united all strands of the US alt-nation, topping the Billboard chart, going five-times platinum and seeing singles like 'Freak On A Leash' requested so many times on MTV's *Total Request Live* that the network 'retired' them from the show.

None of this success appeared to mollify Korn vocalist Jonathan Davis, who sounded so relentlessly anguished that he was reduced/elevated to screaming in tongues. The movement that they spawned/that spawned them came and went, yet Korn have ploughed on to the current day, staying true to their crossover roots by recruiting arena-filling electronic dance music (EDM) producer Skrillex (tellingly, a former metal singer) to contemporise their 2011 album *The Path Of Totality*.

Sadly, his input failed to reverse their falling sales. Still, Korn represent the zenith of nu-metal. It's possible that sounds like faint praise. That is because it is.

LIMP BIZKIT

America's millennial nu-metal scene had more than its fair share of opportunists, and Limp Bizkit were the biggest chancers of all.

Even their big break was jammy: Florida tattooist and Bizkit vocalist Fred Durst inked one of Korn, who were the musical template for his own band, and persuaded him to pass a demo on to his label bosses. Despite the fact that Limp Bizkit just sounded like hoary old power metal with testosterone-driven raps bolted on as a fashion accessory, they got signed up and began non-stop touring with a host of better, more original bands: House of Pain, Deftones, Faith No More.

This paying of dues plus MTV support for the bone-headed single 'Nookie' powered their second album, 1999's *Significant Other*, to number 1 in the US. It was to go on to sell seven million copies.

However, its stellar success was not reflected in its critical notices, as reviewers queued up to mock its repetitive riffing, spirited but amateurish raps and Durst's self-infatuated brooding. Despite his macho front this mockery cut the singer to the quick, and Limp Bizkit's third album, the scatologically titled *Chocolate Starfish And The Hot Dog Flavored Water*, was essentially one extended, truculent whinge at tastemakers' failure to recognise the group's untrammelled magnificence.

On lowest-common-denominator rap-metal workouts like 'My Generation' and 'Rollin'', Durst's cartoon rebellion was truly risible: the veteran US rock critic Bill Holdship noted glumly that the most used words on the record were 'fuck', 'shit', 'motherfucker', 'Limp Bizkit' and the album's unwieldy title, which about summed things up.

With Durst's credibility at subterranean levels, Limp Bizkit's subsequent album sales fell away. His posing as America's oldest, dumbest and most entitled teenager had been only too convincing.

118   01
Td
Tenacious D

TENACIOUS D

Just as a chart countdown leads to number 1, so this Periodic Table of heavy rock happily climaxes with the seminal, self-anointed Greatest Band On Earth: Tenacious D.

Far funnier even than the unintentional low comedy of Limp Bizkit, the bodacious duo of actors Jack Black and Kyle Gass have been linking up as 'the D' since 1994, way before the hit movies *High Fidelity* and *School of Rock* catapulted Black into the Hollywood stratosphere.

An overriding theme links both the movies and Tenacious D: Black's insatiable, child-like love of hard rock, an endearing quality that elevates 'the D', alongside *This Is Spinal Tap* and Steel Panther, to the pantheon of the rare comedy-rock jokes that bear repeating and revisiting.

Dude, how heavy are Tenacious D? At first, not very heavy at all: the initial gag was that Black and Gass were hopeless losers, an 'acoustic metal' duo blind to the oxymoronic nature of that description. They began as an occasional item in an HBO TV sketch series, *Mr. Show*, before getting their own comedy series... and a recording contract.

By the time of their 2001 self-named debut album, the D were a full-blown band with Dave Grohl on drums, and in-between some hit-and-miss skits, they rocked. Hard. A movie and accompanying soundtrack album, *The Pick Of Destiny*, followed, which confirmed that Tenacious D are best when heaviest and most puerile: 'Twas I who fucked the dragon/Fuckalise sing fuckaloo' warbled Black in a shrill falsetto for the epic guff of 'Kickapoo'.

It worked because Black and Gass clearly knew the raucous, roustabout stuff they were churning out was the basest of metals, but they loved it anyway. Endearingly, the mock-heroic rock gods who round off this table sound entirely in their element.

Index

Acknowledgements

Thanks to Laura, for her patience and understanding re lost emails, and to Chris and Flo, for the use of their mansion.